EIGHT PLAYS OF
U.S. HISTORY

THE **G**LOBE **R**EADER'S **C**OLLECTION

EIGHT PLAYS OF U.S. HISTORY

GLOBE FEARON

Pearson Learning Group

Executive Editor: Barbara Levadi
Senior Editor: Bernice Golden
Editors: Helene Avraham, Laura Baselice, Robert McIlwaine
Editorial Assistant: Kristen Shepos
Product Development: PubWorks, Inc.
Production Manager: Penny Gibson
Senior Production Editor: Linda Greenberg
Production Editor: Walt Niedner
Marketing Manager: Sandra Hutchison
Electronic Page Production: The Wheetley Company, Inc.
Cover Design: The Wheetley Company, Inc.
Cover Art: Grant Wood's *Farm Landscape* SuperStock, Inc.
© 1995 Estate of Grant Wood/Licensed by VAGA, New York, NY
Illustrations: Corey Wilkinson

ISBN 0-8359-1374-0
Printed in the United States of America

6 7 8 9 10   06 05 04 03 02

1-800-321-3106
www.pearsonlearning.com

CONTENTS

READING HISTORICAL FICTION PLAYS   **1**

A MAN I KNOW NAMED WILLIAM   **7**
by Eson C. Kim

> Two enslaved Africans in Massachusetts hear the talk
> of freedom during the American Revolution. For Betty
> and William, the only hope for freedom is to run
> away. Then a slave woman named Mum Bett sues for
> her freedom in court. Betty and William must decide
> what to do.

THREE SISTERS by Krista Kanenwisher   **35**

> For many years, Native Americans were supposed to
> learn "white ways." Many of them asked: How impor-
> tant is it to be yourself? Are there advantages to
> becoming more like everyone else? For the members
> of one Native American family, these questions were a
> matter of life or death.

FIGHTING FOR FREEDOM by Wiley M. Woodard   **59**

> Massachusetts was the first state to recruit blacks into
> the Union Army. William and Aaron, two free African
> Americans, are glad to have the opportunity to fight
> for their freedom. But the price of freedom is high.

THE TRIAL OF SACCO AND VANZETTI   **79**
by Rafaela Ellis

> Nicola Sacco and Bartolomeo Vanzetti, two Italian
> immigrants, stand trial for murder. However, their
> trial is about much more than murder. It is about prej-
> udice and the freedom to express ideas. This play is
> based on an actual trial in 1921.

DUST BOWL JOURNEY by Carroll Moulton   107

We often hear of the courage of immigrants who left
their homes to settle in the United States. But what
about the Americans who left the Midwest in the
1930s to settle in California? The Bergman family
must leave their home in Kansas in order to survive.
Their journey west becomes a test of their courage.

HELP WANTED by Joyce Haines   133

The shortage of men in the work force during World
War II led to a big change in the American workplace.
Women left their kitchens for assembly lines. They
made everything from shoes and belts to tanks.
Rosemary and her factory friends find equal work, but
equal opportunity is another story.

THE AMACHE TRAP by Sandra Widener   155

Imagine being forced to leave your neighborhood,
your friends, and your home. "It couldn't happen to
me," you might think. But if it did, what would you
do? This happened to Japanese Americans on the
West Coast during World War II. Share this experience with the Goto family, and find out what they do.

THE FRUITS OF PROTEST by Carroll Moulton   177

Gloria Rodriguez is the daughter of a Mexican
American farm worker. Her father wants her to go to
college. But she gets involved in the farm workers'
struggle for better pay and working conditions. Her
involvement gives Gloria a new pride in her culture
and identity. With her new pride come hard decisions.

READING HISTORICAL FICTION PLAYS

Did you know that the TV series "Little House on the Prairie" and the movie *Schindler's List* were based on events that actually happened? These dramas used history—events that happened in real life. They also mixed in some elements of fiction—stories that are made up. Such works are called *historical fiction*.

The plays you are about to read also blend history with fiction. These plays contain historical facts and events. They show American life as it really was. They have true-to-life settings. The plays are like snapshots of important moments in our nation's past. Many of the characters, though, and the words they say, are made up.

How to Read a Play

Imagine people sitting in a theater blindfolded. They would see neither the stage settings nor the actors. Such an audience would have to rely only on what it could hear. The costumes, the actors' gestures, and the expressions on their faces would not be appreciated. When you read the plays in this book, don't be blind-folded. Keep your eyes and ears open. Even when you read silently, try to make a picture of the stage in your mind's eye. Here are some ways to help you train and use your imagination.

1. Stage Setting When the curtain goes up and the play begins, you have a *stage setting* before you. The playwright uses *stage directions* to describe the set for you. These stage directions are usually printed on the page in *italics*.

Think about the stage set as if you were visiting a new place for the first time. What are your first impressions? What kind of people live here? What sort of action might take place here?

This stage direction from the last act of *The Trial of Sacco and Vanzetti* gives a critical clue about whom the audience should notice first:

> *Sacco's jail cell at the Charlestown Prison, 1927. Sacco and his wife sit on Sacco's cot, holding hands. In the far corner of the room, Vanzetti and Moore are seen talking quietly. Occasionally, Vanzetti and Moore look over at the Saccos, shake their heads, and look away. The spotlight shines on Sacco and his wife.*

2. Exposition The beginning of a play suddenly plunges you into other people's lives. You will naturally have questions about these people. Who are they? What are their relationships to one another? What are their problems? How did these problems happen? You can usually answer these questions in several ways. One way is to read the opening dialogue carefully. Dialogue is the conversation among the people in a play.

For example, what do you learn from the opening dialogue in *Help Wanted*? This conversation shows you that Rosemary, Sue, and the other women are working at an ammunition factory during World War II. The women are not used to factory work. The factory management has hired them only because it is wartime and they are needed. These facts are part of the play's *exposition*, or background.

In *Fighting for Freedom*, you will discover from dialogue how Aaron and William want to help the Union Army to fight against slavery in the Civil War. Their friend Marcus, though, wants nothing to do with a "white man's war."

3. Characters The people in a play are its *characters*. Your first impression of them often comes from what you *see*, not what you *hear*. The clothes that a character wears may tell you something important before a single word is spoken. For example, in *Three Sisters*, Father wears Western clothes, whereas Mother is dressed in Native American style. Using these clues, you can guess each character's opinion of their children's boarding school.

As the play unfolds, you learn more about the characters' relationships. Close attention should be paid to what they say to each other and how they act around each other. To understand a character better, focus on his or her needs and goals. Read these descriptions of William and Betty, the two characters in *A Man I Know Named William*. Even before they begin speaking, you can guess that they will have differing points of view about life:

> *William is raking the hay into a pile and*
> *gathering stray tools. He is a man of about*
> *forty, well-built and lean. He is serious*
> *about his work and something of a loner.*
> *Betty enters wearing a plain house dress.*
> *She is a young woman in her twenties who*

> *is very direct and straightforward but also
> very eager for approval and acceptance.
> There is a sad uneasiness about her, indicat-
> ing discomfort with her new surroundings.*

4. Plot The events that happen in a play are called
the *plot*. These events are not random. One event leads
logically to another, forming the action. The action is
always built around a problem or struggle. This is
called a *conflict*.

There are several different kinds of conflict in the
plays you are about to read. For example, a play can
show an outer conflict. In *The Amache Trap*, the Goto
family struggles against the bias toward Japanese
Americans. In *Fighting for Freedom*, there is a struggle
between the North and the South. Sometimes an outer
conflict is between people and a force of nature. In
Dust Bowl Journey, terrible dust storms cause hardships for the characters. The family in the play, the
Bergmans, must also struggle to be accepted by other
people in a new home.

Finally, a play can show a struggle going on within
an individual. Gloria Rodriguez is faced with an inner
conflict in *The Fruits of Protest*. She must choose
between going to college and working for the rights of
migrant workers.

Keep conflict in mind as you read the plays in this
book. Watch for situations in which characters have
both outer and inner conflicts. The interaction between
Betty and William, the African slaves in *A Man I Know
Named William*, are an example of this. Each has to
choose between running away or remaining a slave.
Each has private doubts about doing either.

There are some questions to ask about conflict as the
action unfolds. What are the characters struggling

against? What are they struggling for? Is the main character fighting for a goal, for an ideal, or for life itself?

The conflicts in a play finally reach a point of greatest tension. This is called the *climax*. The climax of a play is a turning point. The main character must make an important decision or take decisive action. This decision or action usually resolves the conflicts and leads directly to the conclusion.

The climax in *Fighting for Freedom* comes when the men of the Fifty-fourth Regiment charge the parapet of Fort Wagner. This action is what Aaron and William expect all through the play. The conflict is resolved. The next scene answers some remaining questions and concludes the story.

See if you can find the climax of each of the other seven plays in this book. See if you can pick out the main character, and focus on his or her needs and goals. Discover the moment of crisis in the play. You'll enjoy these dramas just as much as your favorite television shows!

A Man I Know Named William

Eson C. Kim

How would you feel if people around you were talking about freedom and independence, and you were enslaved? This was the sad status of African slaves in America during the Revolutionary War. All around them, colonists discussed freedom from Great Britain. There was little interest in freedom for slaves. The Declaration of Independence did not mention slaves.

During the war, some slaves fought with the British forces. Britain offered them freedom. Lord Dunmore, the royal governor of Virginia, formed a brigade of runaway slaves. It was called the Ethiopian Brigade.

Beginning in 1777, some colonies, and later, states, freed slaves. In Massachusetts, a slave woman named Mum Bett sued her owner for cruel treatment. She won her freedom in court. Soon after, all slaves in that state were freed.

In A Man I Know Named William, we meet William and Betty, two African slaves in Massachusetts. Their lives have reached a turning point. The future holds many surprises for them.

VOCABULARY WORDS

heed (HEED) to pay close attention to
❖ The children were wise to *heed* their parents' warnings about the thin ice on the lake.

militia (muh-LIHSH-uh) an army of citizens, rather than professional soldiers, called up in emergencies.
❖ The local *militia* defended the colony during crises.

distractedly (dih-STRAKT-uhd-lee) without paying full attention
❖ "I didn't really mean what I just said," he remarked *distractedly*.

pensive (PEHN-sihv) deeply thoughtful
❖ Although Sally is usually full of fun, that afternoon she was *pensive* and withdrawn.

somber (SAHM-buhr) gloomy, sad
❖ When we visited Jack in the hospital, we found him in a *somber* mood.

despondently (dih-SPAHN-duhnt-lee) hopelessly
❖ He spoke so *despondently* about the future that we tried to cheer him up.

KEY WORDS

Minutemen the American citizen army during the Revolution, ready at a minute's notice
❖ The *Minutemen* resisted the British at the Battles of Lexington and Concord in April 1775.

Thomas Paine American patriot and writer
❖ The most famous pamphlet written by *Thomas Paine* for the Revolution was "Common Sense."

Phillis Wheatley African American poet
❖ *Phillis Wheatley* was the slave of a Boston merchant.

CHARACTERS

Betty, *an enslaved African*
William, *an enslaved African*

SETTING

Act One
Scene 1
Courtyard right outside the stables on Mr. Samuel Whitecombe's Massachusetts estate, early April 1775

Scene 2
Stable courtyard, September 1775

Scene 3
Stable courtyard, November 1775

Act Two
Stable courtyard, July 1776

Act Three
Scene 1
Stable courtyard, 1781

Scene 2
Wooded area far from the estate, later the same day

ACT ONE, SCENE 1

 *An area in front of the stables. At center, the double wooden doors (often left ajar) to the stables. At left, a wooden fence with a water trough in front. At right, a wooden workbench. All the wood is weather-beaten and faded. Neat piles of hay sit in either corner.*

William is raking the hay into a pile and gathering stray tools. He is a man of about forty, well-built and lean. He is serious about his work and something of a loner. Betty enters wearing a plain house dress. She is

a young woman in her twenties who is very direct and straightforward but also very eager for approval and acceptance. There is a sad uneasiness about her, indicating discomfort with her new surroundings.

BETTY: Are you William?

WILLIAM: *(not looking at her)* Yup. Who's asking?

BETTY: *(without emotion)* Betty. Betty's my name.

WILLIAM: What you want with old William?

BETTY: Mrs. Whitecombe wants her carriage ready first thing in the morning. She's taking the little ones to town.

(As she is speaking, William turns to face her. He shows more interest.)

WILLIAM: You're the new house-girl, right?

BETTY: Yes. Yes, I am.

WILLIAM: You don't like it here, do you?

BETTY: What makes you think that?

WILLIAM: I've seen enough comings and goings to know lots of things.

BETTY: I'm just not used to it, that's all. I lived all my life with the Reynoldses, and I need time to feel at home with the Whitecombes.

WILLIAM: Sounds like you was happy with your old master.

BETTY: *(more lively)* Oh yes. But then Master Reynolds died, and I was sent away. I was willed to Master Whitecombe. I was never so sad in my life as I was when I left the Reynoldses' house.

WILLIAM: What's so special about that place? You was a slave there just the same.

BETTY: I found my best friend, Miss Isabelle, there. She taught me things.

WILLIAM: What did a slave have to teach you that you didn't already know?

BETTY: Oh, she wasn't a slave. She was the master's daughter.

WILLIAM: Well, what kinds of things did she teach you to make you wish to be back there so bad?

BETTY: *(hesitating)* You have to promise not to tell anybody.

WILLIAM: Who'd I tell out here? the horses?

BETTY: You have to promise anyway.

WILLIAM: All right. I'll make your silly promise. Now go ahead.

BETTY: Well, I know how to read. Miss Isabelle taught me on the sly. We even studied together a lot.

WILLIAM: Well, that's not gonna be a secret once people hear you speak. Does Master Whitecombe know?

BETTY: He never asked me anything about the Reynoldses. He just said he was my new master and I should heed his word.

WILLIAM: Well, he's not gonna be celebrating over a slave who can read. That's for sure. You better keep quiet about this learning of yours.

BETTY: Tell me, William. You think one of the Whitecombe children will take a fancy to teaching me where Miss Isabelle left off?

WILLIAM: You're not gonna find any Whitecombe inter-ested in giving anything to a slave except orders.

(During the dialogue William has stopped working. Now he returns to it, gathering some stray tools.)

BETTY: Well, maybe I'll do a little studying on my own. You know they have a big library in there. Bigger than the Reynoldses'. I have to get in there somehow.

WILLIAM: Have you got your head on wrong or some-thing? You know what happens if they find you with your nose in a book?

BETTY: I know but—

WILLIAM: For a girl who did so much learning, it seems you didn't do enough thinking to go with it.

BETTY: I don't know why you have to be so jumpy. I can look out for myself, you know.

WILLIAM: *(looking straight at her)* It's not good for any of us when one slave gets whipped.

BETTY: *(pause)* You ever been whipped?

WILLIAM: *(nodding)* I was about as old as you, maybe a bit younger.

BETTY: I never been. Whipped, I mean.

WILLIAM: I never been since then neither. One time's enough to set anybody straight.

BETTY: Soon, we won't have to worry any more about whippings or beatings.

WILLIAM: What nonsense are you talking now?

BETTY: I'm talking about when we get free.

WILLIAM: The more you talk, the more I think you don't know a thing.

BETTY: I do know, William. In the house I hear them talking, and I make sure to mind what they say. Most times they forget I'm around.

WILLIAM: What do those white folks got to say that makes you so sure freedom's coming our way?

BETTY: Even before I came here, Miss Isabelle told me about these petitions being sent to Congress to give us our rights and to end slavery.

WILLIAM: Even so, I'm still a slave so I guess it didn't count for anything.

BETTY: There are even black Minutemen now, you know.

WILLIAM: So I've heard, but when is the part about my freedom coming in? Those men have something to fight for. I hear about free blacks doing what they please, but I'm not one of them.

BETTY: Would you just listen? At supper last night, I heard Master Whitecombe arguing something fierce with Mrs. Whitecombe about some pamphlet.

WILLIAM: Are you getting to a point any time soon? I got work to do.

BETTY: That pamphlet they were fighting over was Thomas Paine's writing. He writes all these essays, and his new one says that slavery is a sin and that it should be ended right this minute. If people like him—white folks I mean—are telling everyone that slavery is evil, then it's only a matter of time for us.

Freedom's coming around, William. I can feel it. Don't you see? There are choices coming for us soon, places for us to go.

WILLIAM: Girl, there are no choices coming for us. I been a slave a long time, and I've heard that same old story about how close freedom is more times than I can count. But until old Master Whitecombe himself comes in here and says any different, I'm just gonna be some old slave boy who tends to the horses.

BETTY: But you're a man, not a boy, William. You ever thought about that?

(During this scene, the light has gradually faded. We see a flickering light in two windows of the house.)

WILLIAM: *(getting uncomfortable)* You better get back to the big house before they send somebody for you.

BETTY: You know I'm right.

WILLIAM: *(getting frustrated)* All I know is that this talk is gonna get us a couple of bloody backs. Now get going.

BETTY: This talk is going to get us free. That's what.

WILLIAM: I thought I said to get going before I whip you myself. *(Betty leaves reluctantly. William looks after her.)* I remember feeling hope like that. I remember . . .

ACT ONE, SCENE 2

William is in the courtyard, polishing and buffing a saddle. Betty enters with some hesitation and walks around him, watching him work.

WILLIAM: Why are you tip-toeing around me for? I'm not made of glass.

BETTY: Well, I didn't know if you still wanted to be my friend.

WILLIAM: Why's that?

BETTY: You don't remember when you turned all mean on me when I first came here? You've been acting sour ever since. I figured I made you mad.

WILLIAM: You sure did. But I don't hold grudges. Life's too short to hang onto angry feelings.

BETTY: I still don't know why you had to turn on me that way.

WILLIAM: You think all your freedom talk back then was the first time I thought about it? You're crazy if you do. A few years back, I saw a choice coming: I could do some accepting or some running. The more I thought about it, the more I knew I couldn't accept being a slave, but I didn't like running away. You get my meaning?

BETTY: You never decided, then?

WILLIAM: There's no deciding. It's like I was two people. One's always gonna be a slave, and the other's always gonna want freedom. For most of us, there's just no simple accepting or running away, only living.

BETTY: There's a choice for you now. I heard them talking at the table this morning.

WILLIAM: One of these days, all your listening is gonna get us in a heap of trouble.

(William goes into the stable to get a cloth to polish the

saddle.)

BETTY: *(in a louder voice)* They were all worked up about the English.

WILLIAM: *(from inside the stable)* That's news?

BETTY: They were talking about Lord Dunmore, the royal governor in Virginia. He has promised freedom to any slave who comes to fight for the British.

WILLIAM: *(standing just inside the stable door)* Say that again?

BETTY: If you fight for the English, Lord Dunmore is going to make you a free man.

WILLIAM: Free . . .?

BETTY: Yes, free. This is your chance, William. You got some place to go now. You got some place to run to.

WILLIAM: *(overwhelmed)* It's not that easy. I've got to do some thinking.

(William walks out into the courtyard, wiping his hands on a cloth. He has obviously lost interest in polishing the saddle.)

BETTY: What for? All you have to do is go to Lord Dunmore and say "I'm here for the fighting," and he's going to make you a free man.

WILLIAM: Now wait a minute. Let me think, I said.

BETTY: Trust me, William. This is right.

WILLIAM: It's not about trust.

BETTY: Then what is it? I know if I had the same choice, I'd be on my way.

WILLIAM: Well, I don't see that you are jumping to do any running.

BETTY: There's no place for girls like me to go. They won't take me to do any fighting.

WILLIAM: Unless tongues was weapons. *(Betty gives him a sharp eye.)* Well, I got more than myself to think about. If I don't make it, then there's no chance for my Esther and Alice to get free on their own. *(Betty looks at him with surprise. William doesn't notice and turns around to look offstage.)*

WILLIAM: Something's stirring the horses. *(He exits to stables.)*

BETTY: His Esther and Alice? Even old William has a family. It must be nice for them, knowing they have somebody, even if they're far away. It's the knowing that counts. I wish I knew who my family was.

WILLIAM: *(He returns.)* Those horses give me nothing but kicks for my trouble. If it was up to me, I'd . . . *(Betty covers her face with her hands and begins to sob.)* Are those tears I see, Betty? I'm sorry if I was sharp with you.

BETTY: Don't mind me. You're the last person who should be saying sorry to anybody.

WILLIAM: I get all worked up, and I forget about feelings sometimes.

BETTY: No. You're a good man, William, the best I've seen in a long time.

WILLIAM: *(confused but touched)* Well, thank you, Miss Betty.

(There is a pause in the conversation.)

BETTY: Do you think you'll fight for the English?

WILLIAM: I don't know. Fighting battles when I'm not so sure what I'm fighting for . . . That don't feel right.

BETTY: You'll get your freedom—and your family. It makes no difference whose flag you're carrying. Fighting's the best chance that's come in a long time.

WILLIAM: But I still don't know, Betty. I just don't know.

ACT ONE, SCENE 3

William is mending the water trough, putting some new braces on the corners, when Betty enters.

BETTY: How are the horses today?

WILLIAM: Messy as usual.

BETTY: Just like the folks in the big house.

WILLIAM: Where you been these past couple of days? I was beginning to think you'd been sold off.

BETTY: It's been really busy in the house, with Christmas coming and all. I wish you could see the place. It looks really fine.

WILLIAM: *(looking up from his work)* I don't care how the big house looks as long as I get my Christmas dinner.

BETTY: *(laughing)* Oh, William.

WILLIAM: Well, it's the one time of the year we get to eat good with all the fixings, like it should be.

BETTY: But don't you forget that you promised to do some dancing with me after Christmas dinner.

(Betty holds her skirt and moves around the courtyard as though practicing a dance.)

WILLIAM: Why are you so set on dancing with an old man like me, anyway?

BETTY: Because you're my best friend here, that's why.

WILLIAM: *(smiling)* What? A sorry old thing like me? What's that say about you now?

BETTY: You're just trying to get out of dancing, that's all.

WILLIAM: Maybe so. *(laughing)* Maybe so.

BETTY: You know, William. I'm glad you didn't leave to go fight for the English.

WILLIAM: Me, too. There's not much left of Dunmore's "Ethiopian Brigade." If I joined up, Dunmore would've made me dead, not free.

BETTY: Not just because they lost . . . You know what I'm saying?

WILLIAM: Yeah. I know what you're saying. I'm glad I'm here now, too.

BETTY: I wish you could come into the house and see what I did with it. You know, sometimes I dream that I have a house of my own with a garden out back and a white porch in the front where I can do my reading and thinking on cool July nights.

WILLIAM: You really got the need for this reading and writing stuff, don't you?

(He returns to his work on the water trough.)

BETTY: I'm going to be famous some day, just like

Phillis Wheatley. Black and white alike read her poems, you know. And I bet they all know she's got a good head on her shoulders—a head with more words in it than "yes, sir" and "no, sir."

WILLIAM: If there's anybody I know who can put her mind to writing something to get people talking, it's you, girl. You just keep those dreams alive, and they'll come true.

BETTY: I know. Tell me something, William. Why didn't you join the English? You didn't know they were going to lose so badly. All you knew was that Dunmore promised freedom. That was your dream, but you never went.

WILLIAM: Oh, I still got the dream, Betty. It's still there somewhere. If all you said about the English was true, I had to ask myself if it was right to fight for them. I didn't know if it was worth running from the evil here only to sell my soul to another master. Betty?

BETTY: Yes?

WILLIAM: If I decided to just run away, without none of this talk about fighting on sides, would you want to go with me?

BETTY: (*stunned*) Run away? You and me? But where?

WILLIAM: I don't know . . . anywhere. If I have to, then I'll join the fighting.

BETTY: But I can't join the militia. There's no place for me to go.

WILLIAM: Will it matter? You'd be free.

BETTY: Free and lost. That's what I'd be.

WILLIAM: You're the one who's talking about freedom all the time, but you never do anything about it. Don't you want to?

BETTY: Remember what you said—about accepting or running? I was thinking that maybe if I worked really hard, the Whitecombe's would let me do some more learning in their library. They're beginning to like me. I know it.

WILLIAM: They don't care a thing about you. Maybe Miss Isabelle did, but that's not usual. Stop trying to make something from nothing.

BETTY: I can't. I can't run with you.

WILLIAM: If you never planned on running, then why'd you do all this talking from the start?

BETTY: I'm stuck, but you can still find freedom.

WILLIAM: You don't have to be stuck anywhere, Betty.

BETTY: I'm telling you I can't, William. I just can't—I don't want to. What if—

WILLIAM: —what if we get caught? It's only right to be scared. You was right to want to be free, Betty. But you was wrong to think that one day you was gonna be free all of a sudden because someone with a white wig signed some paper in the government. Petitions don't do anything. Only a little bit of courage, lots of luck, and a pair of quick feet count this time.

BETTY: *(nervously)* No. I can't do it. I'm not ready. You might be ready, but I'm not. I'm sorry.

WILLIAM: *(resigned)* Well, I can't make you go with me. Don't worry, Betty. I understand. If it don't feel right to you, then it's just not gonna work, I suppose. *(He starts to leave.)*

BETTY: William, wait! *(He stops.)* When are you going? You won't go before Christmas, will you?

WILLIAM: Don't worry. I've waited years to be ready, a couple more won't hurt much. But I don't want to leave you behind. *(He leaves.)*

ACT TWO

Betty and William are in the stable courtyard. William is repairing the fence to the corral.

BETTY: . . . so this declaration says that the colonies won't stand to be owned by the British from now on. Master Whitecombe was all excited, saying how the colonies should be free from tyranny and such. He told his family that there were more hard times coming, but they have to endure for the sake of the greater good.

WILLIAM: So what's this Declaration of Independence say about us slaves?

BETTY: Well, Master Whitecombe didn't mention anything about slaves. But maybe that's because I only caught some of what he was saying before I was called to help in the kitchen.

WILLIAM: No, Betty. You didn't hear anything about blacks in the declaration 'cause there wasn't anything about blacks in it at all. Nothing's gonna change.

BETTY: But we don't know. Maybe they kept real quiet about that part because they knew I was listening. Maybe it's a secret they're keeping from us.

WILLIAM: You think old Master Whitecombe would be sitting at his table sipping his tea with a big old smile if the declaration said slaves was free? He'd be jumping around like he was on fire, no matter who was watching.

BETTY: Even so, Master Whitecombe was talking real serious about something else, too. He said that some colonies were enlisting slaves in their militias, and that others were thinking about it.

WILLIAM: The colonies?

BETTY: Yes. There's going to be a lot more fighting ahead. They're going to need more men.

WILLIAM: (sarcastically) The good old master's never gonna let me go to fight. He can't spare me for a day.

BETTY: Still, you got more places to go now, William. Places that might feel right to you. You got your pick of sides now.

WILLIAM: (distractedly) Yeah. I suppose I got what I was asking for. There's no better time I guess.

BETTY: You got a second chance, and that's no accident. It was meant to be.

WILLIAM: (pensive) Yeah . . .

BETTY: Uh oh. What are you thinking about?

WILLIAM: About you.

BETTY: Me? You have no cause to be thinking about me, I told you.

WILLIAM: I'm still gonna wait for you.

BETTY: Yeah, and watch all these chances pass you

right by? Oh no. Not on account of me.

WILLIAM: I made a promise.

BETTY: And I'm saying that I don't care about that. You just go when you get the chance.

WILLIAM: And this is it?

BETTY: You know that when you run, your best chance is to go alone. My company is not going to help you any. I'd just be trouble.

WILLIAM: We could do it, Betty. I know it.

BETTY: There isn't an ounce of sense in this, William. I don't have a place to go, but you do. I can't run as fast as you can. I can't help you once you're out there. Even if I did want to go, you shouldn't want me to.

WILLIAM: It makes me mad that you're not doing what you want to, deep down inside.

BETTY: William!

WILLIAM: You wanted to go with me last time we talked about it, but you was afraid then, too. You're always gonna be afraid. You're always gonna be a slave—

BETTY: (angry) Maybe I want to be a slave right now. Maybe that's right for me now. And maybe it's not me that's scared, but you.

(She turns to leave.)

WILLIAM: (sobered) Wait. (She stops.) Maybe you're right, like always. These past couple weeks, maybe it wasn't William talking; it was fear. I been making it look like you got the problem. I know you wasn't ready to run, but I kept trying to make you. Then I tried to say I wasn't going without you 'cause it was better to say that than to say, "Betty, I'm not running now 'cause I'm scared to go."

BETTY: *(softening)* You'll be free, William. There's no doubting that.

WILLIAM: I don't know. Sometimes I wake up in the morning and ask myself: "Am I ever gonna be a man, or am I gonna be some slave boy my whole life?"

BETTY: You're a man, William. Don't let anybody tell you different. *(Betty goes to leave.)* Just remember, when you're ready to leave, you just go! I'm not holding you to that silly promise you made. It's all you now, like it should be.

ACT THREE, SCENE 1

Betty is sitting on the ground, leaning up against the stable doors. She is staring out in front of her with a blank, lost stare of complete despair, when William enters. He takes off his jacket, apparently returning from some errand.

WILLIAM: I got something to tell you.

BETTY: *(distracted and somber)* Yeah?

WILLIAM: You won't believe it.

BETTY: *(still distant)* Yeah . . .?

WILLIAM: *(He looks at her.)* Hey. What's got into you?

BETTY: Nothing.

WILLIAM: No, it's something. I can see it. You look about as white as Master Whitecombe himself.

BETTY: It's nothing. No feelings at all for a nobody like me.

WILLIAM: What is this talk? What's wrong with you?

BETTY: I told you.

WILLIAM: What made you all sad like this? That mean Mrs. Whitecombe hit you or something?

BETTY: She never touched me, but I'm all beat up inside. I feel like I'm never getting up from here.

WILLIAM: Betty, tell me what's going on. You heard some news, didn't you? *(no response)* Didn't you?

BETTY: *(hoarsely)* Yeah. I got some news.

WILLIAM: Bad?

BETTY: *(despondently)* Mr. McHenry came to see Master Whitecombe this morning. He said that he didn't know what this world was coming to if they were going to allow slaves to question their masters.

WILLIAM: Was there an uprising somewhere?

BETTY: No. No uprising. Just a slave woman named Mum Bett.

WILLIAM: Mum Bett?

BETTY: She is suing for her freedom today—in court. Mr. McHenry said they even told her master he had to pay her some money for her suffering.

WILLIAM: Well, there's some good news for a change. *(looks back at Betty)* It's not good news to you?

BETTY: Good? What's so good about being a slave still? What's so good about thinking all this time you don't have a place to go and someone else goes and makes a place for herself while you sat back like some fool?

WILLIAM: Come on. You're no fool.

BETTY: Mum Bett never learned to read, but she still has enough sense to know how to fight for her freedom. She's making her own way.

WILLIAM: And you'll make yours in time.

BETTY: Time means nothing. Some people just don't have what it takes to get what they want. They're not strong enough. It's got nothing to do with time or learning.

WILLIAM: Mum Bett's nothing special. I bet you she got a bad case of the shakes just like any slave fighting a master for freedom.

BETTY: But she's doing it. And maybe she's going to be free.

WILLIAM: And you will be, too. Look. You can't go talking like this. What about your reading and your writing? Don't you want to write those essays and poems like Thomas Paine and Phillis Wheatley?

BETTY: That was the young Betty talking, the one that didn't know any better than to go talking nonsense about things that can't ever happen.

WILLIAM: That was the Betty that knew she had dreams and knew she was made for a smarter place than waiting on some spoiled white folks.

BETTY: I thought I was something, William. Just because I could read somebody's leftover school books, I thought that made me something else. I thought I was so special that freedom was just going to come to me one day. But you were right, William.

Petitions don't matter, and there's no magic waiting to happen to me or to any of us.

WILLIAM: That's why we have to make some magic of our own. At least I'm gonna try. Look at me, Betty. Take a good, long look because I can't promise when I can see you again. I'm gonna run. Tonight.

BETTY: *(shocked into attention)* You're running? Tonight?

WILLIAM: I made the choice.

BETTY: What if you can't find work? What if they catch you? You don't have any money. You don't have anything.

WILLIAM: If things get too tight, then I'll look to do some fighting. But that's only if I find myself caught in a tight spot. Look. I'm heading for Vermont. I hear there're people there who'll help me. I got to go real soon. But you just remember something. When I get my freedom, I'm coming back for you, just like for my Esther and Alice. And I'll be my own man.

BETTY: William, I—

WILLIAM: There's no time to get all messy with crying now. I'm already behind. You just keep practicing all that reading and writing, so when I come back for you, you'll be good and ready to teach me.

BETTY: I didn't know you wanted to learn how to read.

WILLIAM: Well, I have to learn so I can read your stuff some day, don't I? Now give me a hug to warm me on this cold night, and let me get on my way before I change my mind. *(They hug.)* Bye, girl.

(He tears himself away and leaves.)

BETTY: Bye . . . William . . .

(She sinks to the ground and stares at the floor of the lonely courtyard.)

ACT THREE, SCENE 2

A small clearing in a wooded area at twilight. William enters stage running, then takes a rest. He is nervous and fearful but also determined.

BETTY: *(from offstage)* William?

(William jumps up, startled into attention. Betty enters, and he relaxes.)

WILLIAM: Betty! What are you doing here?

BETTY: Oh, William. I found you.

WILLIAM: How did you know—

BETTY: After you left, I didn't feel right. I couldn't stay behind. I was going to run my own way, but then I had to find you. I had to tell you that I was going to run for my freedom, too. Even if I was scared. You were right about one thing. I couldn't sit around waiting for what I want. If people are going to know my name some day, they're going to know the name of a free woman, not some slave girl.

WILLIAM: *(with pride)* I believe it more than ever now.

BETTY: I know there isn't time to talk now. You got to keep moving. But I just had to let you know. *(goes to leave)*

WILLIAM: You mean you're not coming with me?

BETTY: *(stops)* You know we have a better chance—

a much better chance—if we're apart.

WILLIAM: I know. But let's go a little ways together. Just for a short while. We got this far already.

BETTY: Okay. It's more lonely at night. It'll be good to have somebody to run with until morning.

WILLIAM: I guess we finally did it, Betty. After all this time.

BETTY: I never thought we would.

WILLIAM: Even when we go our own ways, I promise that you'll look into these eyes again. One day, I'll come calling when you least expect it.

BETTY: You've been good to me, William.

WILLIAM: And you been good to me, girl.

BETTY: Even if I don't make it, I'm never going to be sorry for trying.

WILLIAM: *(smiling)* We already made it. The minute we said "no more" to the "yes, sirs" and the "no, sirs," we made it.

BETTY: And when I get down to some serious writing, the world's going to see through my eyes. They're going to know everything about a writer named Betty and the man I know named William.

WILLIAM: Now that'll be a blessed day for us both. *(They run into the woods together.)*

READING FOR UNDERSTANDING

Overview

1. Where and when does the action of the play take place?

2. What big decision do William and Betty discuss during the play? What does each character finally decide to do?

Act One

3. Why does Betty miss the Reynoldses' house? Why is she hopeful that an end to slavery will come soon?

4. Who is Lord Dunmore? What offer has he made to the slaves?

5. What does Betty tell William about her ambition in life? Why isn't she ready to join William in a run for freedom?

Act Two

6. What effect does the failure of the Declaration of Independence to mention the slaves have on William and Betty?

7. In this act, how does William explain his own reluctance to run away?

Act Three

8. Why does Betty say, "Maybe I want to be a slave right now"?

9. What news does Betty tell William about Mum Bett? How does this news make her feel now about her own actions?

10. In what ways has Betty affected William's thoughts on running away?

11. Why do William and Betty decide to stick together?

RESPONDING TO THE PLAY

1. Imagine that you are either William or Betty. Reread the three scenes of Act One. Then write a short diary entry giving your reactions to the other character *(Betty or William)* up to this point in the play. In your entry, tell what you like and dislike about her/him.

2. Betty has very clear ideas about her ambitions in life. Her goals are connected to one of her heroines, the poet Phillis Wheatley. What are your career goals? Is there any connection between these goals and one of your personal heroes or heroines? Explain in a paragraph.

REVIEWING VOCABULARY

Match each word on the left with the correct definition on the right.

1. heed	**a.** hopelessly
2. somber	**b.** citizen army
3. pensive	**c.** without paying full attention
4. despondently	**d.** to pay close attention
5. distractedly	**e.** American citizen army
6. minutemen	**f.** deeply thoughtful
7. militia	**g.** gloomy

THINKING CRITICALLY

1. Throughout the play, what does the author reveal about the experience of being a slave?

2. What are some of the reasons that William hesitates for so long to make a run for freedom? What are some of the reasons that Betty hesitates?

3. What is the most important turning point for each character in his or her decision to run away?

4. Mum Bett once said, "Anytime while I was a slave, if one minute's freedom had been offered to me, and I had been told I must die at the end of that minute, I would have taken it." Do you think that William and Betty would agree with this statement by the end of the play? Explain why or why not.

WRITING PROJECTS

1. Assume that Betty and William escape successfully. Years later, when Betty has become a writer, she meets Mum Bett, whose name is now Elizabeth Freeman. Write a short account of the meeting, using Betty's first-person point of view. Be sure to include a comment about how important Mum Bett's lawsuit was to Betty.

2. The world sometimes seems divided between idealists who look at life as it should be, and realists, who look at life as it really is. In this play, who is the idealist and who is the realist? Or do both William and Betty have a bit of each in them? Write a paragraph or two to explain your answer.

Three Sisters

Krista Kanenwisher

Someday you will choose where you would like to live. You probably wouldn't want the government to decide for you. More than 100 years ago, the U.S. government told Native Americans they had to live in special areas by themselves. These areas were called reservations.

The government also wanted to control what young Native Americans learned. It wanted Native Americans to learn "white ways." For this reason, some Native American children were forced to go to boarding schools. White people ran these schools.

How important is it to be yourself? What are the advantages of being like everyone else? In the play you are about to read, the members of a Native American family have different answers to these questions.

VOCABULARY WORDS

cisterns (SIHS-ternz) large water tanks
❖ The fort had *cisterns* of water.

forlorn (fawr-LAWRN) miserable, wretched
❖ Her sad eyes told us that she felt *forlorn*.

livid (LIHV-ihd) red with anger or rage
❖ Mr. Webster was *livid* over the stolen car.

switch (SWIHTCH) to whip with a stick as a form of punishment
❖ Teachers used to *switch* students who misbehaved.

corset (KAWR-siht) a close-fitting undergarment worn by women to mold the figure
❖ That description of a *corset* makes it sound most uncomfortable!

curtsy (KERT-see) a greeting of respect in which a girl or woman bends her knees and lowers her body
❖ A *curtsy* is now regarded as old-fashioned.

infirmary (ihn-FER-muh-ree) a room or building in a school or other institution that serves as a hospital
❖ We took the sick children to the school *infirmary*.

elocution (ehl-uh-KYOO-shuhn) the art of public speaking
❖ To speak well in public, you must study *elocution*.

quarantined (KWAHR-uhn-teend) isolated from other people in order to keep a disease from spreading
❖ The victims of the plague were *quarantined*.

KEY WORD

pox (PAHKS) short for chicken pox or smallpox, diseases that often spread among children
❖ The child had a fever and rash from the *pox*.

CHARACTERS

Three Native American sisters:
    Alice, *fourteen years old*
    Vivian, *sixteen years old*
    Lucy, *thirteen years old*
Mr. Hayes, *school superintendent*
William, *student*
Peter, *student*
Mrs. Graham, *school matron*
Mother
Father, *tribal chief*

SETTING

A Play in One Act

Scene 1

The home economics room of the school

Scene 2

The lawn in front of the school

SCENE 1

***B**oarding school* for *Native Americans in the late 1800s. The home economics room. This room has a long food preparation table, cisterns for water, and an open pantry with roll-out drawers of flour and sugar on one side of the room, balanced on the other side by a pedal sewing machine and fabric table. An ironing board is positioned next to a potbellied stove. Alice and Vivian are at the table, rolling out dough for biscuits. Lucy is at the ironing board. While Lucy irons, Alice and Vivian make enough biscuits for the entire girls' dorm.*

ALICE: *(Alice and Vivian look accusingly at Lucy.)* It is just too bad that we are in here at four o'clock in the morning making biscuits when we could be sleeping in our beds!

(Lucy continues her work at the ironing board without looking up.)

ALICE: Lucy, wouldn't you like to be sleeping in your bed?

(Lucy turns slightly from her sisters and looks forlorn.)

VIVIAN: Leave her alone, Alice. It was priceless, seeing the expression on Mrs. Graham's face when you told her what Lucy said. She looked livid, perfectly livid.

ALICE: I would never have told her, except that she threatened to switch us in front of the entire school. I'd rather make biscuits at four A.M. than be humiliated in front of everyone.

LUCY: Why, they won't allow us to speak our language here. *(And suddenly in a loud voice directed at Vivian.)* And I hate words like "perfectly livid"! *(Lucy mimics Vivian. Lucy begins to mumble under her breath in her own language.)*

ALICE: *(laughing and mimicking Vivian)* It's true, Vivian, you are a pistol. You put on such a pretense with your "perfectly livid" and "absolutely charming." How have you learned this language so quickly?

VIVIAN: It's all just pretend. Cinch up your corset really tight. *(Vivian sucks in her cheeks and her midriff and pretends to fix her corset.)* Imagine yourself tremendously pale. *(She pats flour on her face.)* And speak with big lips! "Gudt mahning, Mrs. Grawwham, you look perfectly wonderful and tremendously large this mahning."

(Vivian exaggerates every word and pretends to pass out across the biscuits, supposedly from being unable to breathe in her corset. Both Alice and Lucy are laughing at Vivian's antics.)

ALICE: *(urgently, while still laughing)* Vivian! Vivian! Stop it! If Mrs. Graham catches us, we will be making biscuits for a month. *(She suddenly stops laughing.)* Sometimes . . . I wish Mother and Father were here. I don't know why these people are always angry with us. Back home, grownups never treat children the way they do here.

LUCY: Do these people switch their own children?

ALICE: I believe they do. They don't seem to mean ill by it. They feel that this chases the evil out of children.

VIVIAN: Well, that's it then. That's why their children seem to be so nervous.

LUCY: I don't know why the boys are nervous, but I think the girls are nervous because of these corset things. They could explode at any moment. *(Lucy rests a moment against the ironing board, putting her hand to her forehead.)*

ALICE: That reminds me, Lucy, you know it's the rule. You must wear the corset or be punished for indecency! You do have it on, don't you? Lucy, are you all right?

LUCY: *(Sneaking the corset out of a dress pocket from under her apron, Lucy stuffs the corset down the front of her blouse and looks at Alice out of the side of her eyes. The laces are left hanging out of the top of the collar.)* Yes, I have it on. But I hate it. How do the girls ride in these, or breathe, or eat? *(Trying not to* *be noticed, Lucy continues to stuff the corset down the front of her blouse while her back is slightly turned toward her sisters.)*

ALICE: Oh, dear! I just saw Superintendent Hayes go by the window. Get to work. Lucy, no matter how angry you get with him, you must answer him in English!

VIVIAN: I don't think it matters how you answer him. He's deaf as this rolling pin.

MR. HAYES: Good morning, girls. *(The girls nod.)* I believe it is more correct for young ladies to respond with a "Good morning, Mr. Hayes," and a slight curtsy, if you will.

THE SISTERS: Good morning, Mr. Hayes. *(They curtsy.)*

MR. HAYES: Mrs. Graham has told me that you, Lucy, were quite rude. Your remarks were hurtful and brought her to tears. Did you truly mean to say that Mrs. Graham was as large as your mother's cow?

(Vivian and Alice are standing behind Mr. Hayes. They shake their heads so that Lucy can take their hint. In the meantime, Lucy has started to nod yes but glances up in time to follow their lead and shake no.)

MR. HAYES: Well, Lucy, did you mean to say that?

LUCY: No, sir.

(Mr. Hayes turns to leave, but first he advances to Lucy.)

MR. HAYES: Thank goodness for that! I believe a short note of apology will set this thing straight. . . . Lucy, *what* is that thing hanging out of your collar there? *(He points to her corset strings.)* And, Vivian, you must have had such a difficult time with these biscuits that there is flour all over your nose. *(Vivian quickly wipes her face with the skirt of her apron.)* In a short while, Mrs. Graham will send William and Peter up with more supplies. Please make room for them. Lucy, make certain that you mend those pants before passing them on.

(Lucy takes the pants she is ironing and sits down at the sewing machine. She does not look at Mr. Hayes. As Mr. Hayes leaves the room, Lucy sits down in a chair beside the ironing board and begins to cry.)

ALICE: *(She moves toward Lucy, stands behind her, places her hands around her shoulders, and pushes the corset strings back into her blouse.)* Don't cry, Lucy, it's going to be all right. In a few short weeks, we will finally get to go home for the summer. Just hang on and try to stay out of trouble.

LUCY: *(trying not to sob)* This is such an awful place!

ALICE: I will help you with the apology note. That old Mrs. Graham is so mean that she deserved what you said, but we still have to write an apology.

VIVIAN: *(softly)* That's right, Lucy, we'll write an apology and tell Mrs. Graham that you are very sorry that she looks like a cow.

ALICE: Stop it, Vivian! It's that sort of thing that got us into this mess in the first place. Mother and Father don't want us to get into trouble, and they expect us to watch out for one another. We don't have a choice about school.

LUCY: I'm not coming back next year.

VIVIAN: We have to come back because if we don't, the rest of the families on the reservation won't want to send their children here.

LUCY: I'll hide when the reservation superintendent comes to get us.

VIVIAN: Lucy, you can't. The reservation superintendent will punish the other families by taking away their supplies. Some of the people will starve without the supplies.

ALICE: We're lucky; our land has the creek running through it, and we can haul the water we need for the garden.

VIVIAN: Mother's garden is right by the creek, and she can run the water to it. But not everyone can do that, and they have had a lot of difficulty growing their food.

LUCY: Why can't our people live wherever they want like the other settlers?

ALICE: Father has explained all of this before. Just try to get along. *(Vivian has become tearful and wipes her eyes.)* Lucy, look, what you're doing isn't helpful.

LUCY: I can't help how I feel.

ALICE: Hurry, Vivian, help me clean up this flour before Mrs. Graham comes. Lucy, there's some paper on the end of the table. Start to write your note so we can get this over with.

(William and Peter haul in big bags of flour.)

WILLIAM: Here's flour for three troublemakers!

PETER: I made a dancing feather for Lucy.

(Peter gives Lucy a feather, which has a colorful string wrapped around the quill.)

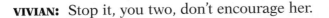

VIVIAN: Stop it, you two, don't encourage her.

WILLIAM: We're not kidding; we think that Lucy is a strong one. And just to prove to you how strong we think she is, we have taken this from the mail sack. *(He pulls out a letter.)*

PETER: You know, since you are in trouble, they keep your mail from home. *(The girls rush to the letter.)*

ALICE: Oh, Peter, what if they find out?

PETER: They won't.

(The girls rush to open their letter, and Vivian reads it aloud.)

VIVIAN: "Dear daughters. We have heard that some children at the school have been sick with the pox. Many parents have had the agency contact the school. They have not answered. We will come to see for ourselves. We should leave on Tuesday and arrive on Thursday. Take care of each other. Your loving parents."

ALICE: When? When are they coming? *(She takes the letter.)* They said Thursday, as in this Thursday, today?

PETER: You won't be allowed to see your parents if you are still in detention.

WILLIAM: We'll help put up the flour and sugar. Then we've got to get out of here. Look, you three! You can't let on you got the letter, or else I'll be making biscuits.

(The boys rush to put away the flour and sugar, and the girls hurry back to their assignments.)

MRS. GRAHAM: Good morning, girls. And a particularly good morning to you, Lucy. Don't you think that the smell of fresh-baked biscuits in the morning is a wonderful thing?

ALICE AND VIVIAN: Yes, Mrs. Graham.

MRS. GRAHAM: Lucy?

LUCY: Yes, Mrs. Graham. *(She walks over with the note.)*

MRS. GRAHAM: An apology. So thoughtful of you, Lucy. What is that string hanging from your collar?

VIVIAN: *(She moves in between Lucy and Mrs. Graham.)* I'll fix it, Mrs. Graham. Poor thing, she's having trouble with her . . . her button.

(Mrs. Graham turns to leave, taking a tray of biscuits with her.)

MRS. GRAHAM: As soon as you have finished the next batch, one of you begin to haul the trays over to the breakfast room. *(She leaves.)*

ALICE: Lucy, I'll iron while you help Vivian. Why don't you start running the trays of biscuits over to the breakfast room while Vivian gets the next batch ready for the oven?

(Lucy hurries a tray of biscuits out of the room, stopping to wipe her brow.)

VIVIAN: Yep. She's gonna run for it, the minute Mother and Father get here. Not a chance of their wagon getting out of here without Lucy!

ALICE: I think you're right. Vivian, I'm really worried about her. She has had a fever for two days, and she doesn't feel very well. I think that's why she's been so upset lately.

VIVIAN: Should we tell someone she is sick?

ALICE: I don't know. But if they know she is getting sick, they will put her in the infirmary with all the other sick children.

VIVIAN: But if she's sick, we have to help her, and that means telling someone.

ALICE: No. She'd never forgive us. But we have to find a way to talk her into letting us help her, at least until she is well.

VIVIAN: Well, don't let her think she might be seriously ill. There's no telling how she might react.

(Lucy returns with the empty pan.)

LUCY: I want Mother and Father to take me home. I'm not giving in to these people. Father will take me back with him.

ALICE: Please don't make this hard on them, Lucy. What do you mean, you are not giving in to these people?

LUCY: Of course, I mean to the school. I don't like these clothes. They're heavy, and these shoes hurt! I like speaking in my own language. I like playing with my friends. I didn't ask to come here. Vivian, come home with me.

VIVIAN: *(She looks away, embarrassed.)* Lucy, I want to stay. It's sort of fun, seeing all the boys and girls. I don't mind the clothes, although I miss Mother and Father.

LUCY: That's just like you, Vivian. You copy everything. You gave in before you got here.

ALICE: You're both right. We shouldn't forget our families. Our ways of living are very different from those at this school. But it's all right, Lucy, if we like these clothes.

LUCY: But why do we have to hide our feelings and our own personal items from home?

VIVIAN: That is a mystery to me.

ALICE: Sometimes, I'm saddened that I've had to hide our pictures or our clothing from home. But Mr. Hayes said that if we keep those things in front of us, we won't be able to learn the better way.

VIVIAN: Why is it a better way?

LUCY: Better how? Is it better that our people leave their homes to grow up in boarding schools without our parents?

ALICE: Why are you asking me?

LUCY: Because you always know what the teachers think!

ALICE: They say these new ways are better. They are civilized ways. But I don't really understand what "civilized" means. They say that it is good we are learning to speak like them and to wear these clothes. We will learn how to behave in polite society. Ouch! *(She has burned herself ironing.)*

VIVIAN: We have so many privileges now. *(laughing)* We can iron our clothes, wear tight shoes, and strain the seeds out of the lemonade. We can sleep in prickly beds, and some of us wear corsets!

ALICE: I do like the piano and singing. And admit it, Lucy, you love lemonade.

LUCY: I just wish we weren't always in trouble. I don't care what old Mrs. Graham says. When the folks come, I'm going to see them whether we are through with our discipline assignments or not. I want to go home, so that I can bathe in the pond, all of me, all at once.

VIVIAN: I do detest those pans. They barely hold any water. Washing yourself using a pan is so awful.

ALICE: *(smiling)* Mother will be surprised when she sees those pans. She will be surprised that we keep ourselves clean with a thimbleful of water. There's so much to show Mother and Father. Lucy, you look flushed. Are you feeling sick?

LUCY: *(dabbing her forehead)* I feel hot. It's just this room. I'll carry two trays this trip. How many more do we have to make?

VIVIAN: We are nearly done. How much more ironing, Alice?

ALICE: Almost done. Just help me fold these last few pillowcases.

(The girls move to fold the last few flat pieces, and then each of them picks up pans of biscuits to carry out.)

SCENE 2

(Stage left) The three girls are sitting out on the lawn in front of the school with their parents. Mother is looking at a book with Vivian and Alice. Father and Lucy are sitting stage right of the others, slightly forward from

the others. Father is sitting with his arm around Lucy. Lucy is upset. Mother is in traditional Native American dress. Father is in a new frontier outfit.

MOTHER: You girls look wonderful. *(She touches their hair and encourages them to turn their heads so she can see the backs of their heads.)* This hair looks so unusual. Why is it knotted underneath?

ALICE: If we run our combs backward and then smooth it down and pin it up, it makes this large poof on top of our head. Do you like it?

MOTHER: Yes, I like it, but I like our braids better. Let me see, are you sewing things on the new machine?

ALICE: I love that machine, Mother; it makes sewing so easy and fast.

VIVIAN: Things last longer and don't break so easily.

MOTHER: Have you tried to sew leather with it?

ALICE: We make everything here with cloth. Our shoes are from eastern states. I'm sure these machines would ruin moccasins.

(They all laugh.)

MOTHER: *(becoming more serious)* Alice, many of the parents have sent us here to find out about their children. When we asked the school superintendent about them, he said that many are busy and cannot talk to us. He hated to tell us, but we already knew many have been very sick.

ALICE: I know there are many children who are sick, but they don't tell us anything about it. If they see someone with a fever, they simply put that student in the infirmary. Lucy has not seen some of her friends for the last week. I am a little worried, Mother.

MOTHER: One of the women who works here as a nurse's aid has sent word home that several of our reservation children have died from the chicken pox. *(The girls look worried and shocked.)*

ALICE: *(angrily)* No wonder the school doesn't tell us about these things.

VIVIAN: Mother, Lucy is unhappy here. But Alice and I like our classes and most of our teachers.

ALICE: We have made good friends in the dorms, and sometimes it is really fun here.

VIVIAN: I am learning to sew and play the piano. And Alice is learning elocution and voice. Both of us are playing basketball. We wouldn't want to go home.

MOTHER: Why is Lucy so unhappy?

VIVIAN: Because she misses you and Father and the farm. I don't think she will ever be happy here.

ALICE: She hates speaking English, and she is always getting extra assignments because she refuses to give up our language.

VIVIAN: Mother, Lucy has been a little sick these past few days.

ALICE: We haven't told anyone because they would send her to the infirmary.

VIVIAN: Also, Lucy refuses to wear her corset. Instead of wearing it, she simply stuffs it down the front of her blouse.

(Father and Lucy have wiped away Lucy's tears. They have moved back to join the other conversation.)

MOTHER: What is this corset?

ALICE: It is something that you wear over your bosom and around your waist.

VIVIAN: It has these bones that stand side by side to each other and are sewn onto the fabric. You wrap it around your middle. There are strings that lace the two ends together. The waist is pulled very tightly, making your bosom look large and your waist small.

LUCY: Actually, Mother, it makes you look like an exploding pear. Here, this is a corset!

(She whips her corset out of her blouse. She's delighted to wave it around, and the family explodes in laughter.)

FATHER: That looks like a terrible thing! Do you store it in the front of your shirt?

ALICE: No, Father, only Lucy stores hers. The rest of us wear it tied around our waist.

FATHER: I was one of the first boys from the reservation to go to the mission school. That was very hard. I remember being puzzled by the hard saddles that the soldiers put on the horses for riding.

VIVIAN: Did they let you speak our language?

FATHER: No. Instead of a Mrs. Graham, we had a mean superintendent of schools. He wouldn't allow us to speak in our language, and he took away our tobacco, which we used for our ceremonies. He had hair all over his body, even his face.

LUCY: Did you drink lemonade?

FATHER: No, but they made this black drink that they called coffee. When I first tasted it, I thought it was poison. But now I like this drink. Like Lucy, I missed my parents and the farm. But I did learn a little. I learned to read and to do some mathematics. Because of that school, I have been able to help our people.

LUCY: Alice and Vivian are going to stay and learn how to help our people, but I am going home. *(The rest of the family moans.)* I mean it; I'm going home. If you don't let me come along with you, I'll just run home on my own! *(Lucy wipes the sweat from her forehead again.)*

MOTHER: Lucy, are you feeling well? You look a little sick. *(Mother looks around in order to make certain that no one is listening.)* Perhaps, if you are sick, we should have the school doctor see you.

THE SISTERS: No!

ALICE: Mother, you must understand that if Lucy is sick they will put her in the infirmary, and she could catch the pox from the others.

FATHER: But if she has the pox, then she must be isolated so that others won't catch it from her.

MOTHER: We are not putting Lucy in the infirmary with the others. If she has the flu, then we will have to put her in a place where she could not get sick with the pox. We'll keep her with us and keep quiet.

VIVIAN: It seems such a terrible choice that we are making. It seems that we are protecting Lucy at the possible expense of others.

MOTHER: But, Vivian, would you have us protect others at the expense of Lucy?

(Mother embraces Lucy. She is sitting behind Lucy and places her arms around her and rocks slightly back and forth.)

FATHER: When the tribe asked me to lead them, you girls were proud. You, Mother, bragged to all of the others that it was right that I should lead our people. Then when the people gave gifts to honor me, you were proud. You liked that. There is always a price that comes with leadership.

VIVIAN: Are you saying that the price is to leave Lucy in the infirmary with the others?

FATHER: The people have sent us here to find out what has happened with their children. We have found that there is a great illness among them. And we have found that Lucy is sick. Look at her face, and feel her skin. A fever has come over her, and her eyes are red.

MOTHER: What are we going to do?

FATHER: We must do what is right. That is the cost of leadership, to do what is right even at your own expense. We cannot take Lucy back with us and put at risk the people on the reservation. The pox is a great epidemic. We must keep her here.

MOTHER: If we cannot take Lucy, then I'll stay here with her.

VIVIAN: Mother, what about our brothers at home? You cannot leave them for so long.

ALICE: Mother, I will go into the infirmary with Lucy. They need some more nursing aides, and I will volunteer. I didn't know that our children from home were so ill. They must be very frightened by the pox.

I'll take Lucy in and stay with her and the others.

(Mr. Hayes enters and crosses the stage to the small family.)

MR. HAYES: What a lovely little family. *(He steps forward to shake hands with Father.)* Hello, sir.

FATHER: Hello, Mr. Hayes. I must have an answer regarding the list of children which I have given you.

MR. HAYES: Terribly sorry for the delay. We will get that for you shortly. *(Mr. Hayes looks carefully at Lucy.)* Lucy, are you ill?

FATHER: Mr. Hayes, Lucy is ill.

(Mr. Hayes immediately backs away. He takes a handkerchief from his pocket and wipes his hands. He shields his nose and mouth with it.)

MR. HAYES: I must confess that the children have had an outbreak of the pox. We have lost several children, but we have not notified their parents because we were worried that the other parents would rush to remove their children. Many children have already been exposed. Lucy will have to be quarantined. You folks will have to camp outside of the school grounds and stay close for at least ten days before you will be allowed to return home.

FATHER: Alice will stay in the infirmary to care for Lucy and the other children from our reservation. Their parents must receive word of their illness or death.

MR. HAYES: I must warn you folks that if Alice goes in with Lucy, she cannot come out when Lucy is well unless she has had the pox or until the epidemic is over. Otherwise, she might infect the rest of the children.

VIVIAN: We should probably send someone into the infirmary who is of hearty stock, like Mrs. Graham.

MR. HAYES: Vivian!

(The family move to embrace one another one last time. Then Father moves back, as Mother holds onto the girls. Alice walks with her arm around Lucy, and they follow Mr. Hayes across the campus to the infirmary.)

MOTHER: Will we camp here for ten days?

FATHER: We will camp. Maybe when we go home, we can take our people more news of their children. Maybe we will know Lucy is safe. Alice will not be safe for a long time. We must not cry. It's a bad omen if we cry.

MOTHER: I won't cry. But for many days my heart will be on the ground.

(In the distance, Vivian is seen walking away. She turns and waves to her parents. They slowly wave back, and then they turn to leave.)

———————————

READING FOR UNDERSTANDING

The following paragraphs summarize the play. Decide which of the words below the paragraphs best fits in each blank. Write your answers on a separate sheet of paper.

Alice, Vivian, and Lucy are three **(1)**_____ who attend a Native American boarding **(2)**_____. Because Lucy is rude to Mrs. Graham, the girls are **(3)**_____ by having to make **(4)**_____. Mr. Hayes, the school **(5)**_____, tells Lucy that she must write a note of **(6)**_____. Two **(7)**_____ named William and Peter bring the sisters a **(8)**_____ from their parents.

The sisters learn the news that some children at the school are ill with the **(9)**_____. Alice worries that Lucy may be taken to the **(10)**_____ because she has a **(11)**_____. Lucy tells Alice and Vivian that she is **(12)**_____ at school and wants their parents to take her **(13)**_____. She hates wearing the school **(14)**_____ and always speaking English rather than her own **(15)**_____. When their parents **(16)**_____, they learn of Lucy's unhappiness.

As the tribal **(17)**_____, the girls' father feels that they have a **(18)**_____ to remain at the school and do the right thing. Father says that Lucy must be **(19)**_____ if she has the pox. Alice offers to go to the infirmary with Lucy to care for her and for the other sick children from the **(20)**_____.

Words: *biscuits, home, clothes, sisters, apology, letter, pox, school, punished, fever, students, superintendent, chief, reservation, infirmary, unhappy, language, isolated, arrive, responsibility*

RESPONDING TO THE PLAY

1. Lucy does not like the school. But Vivian explains that the other families on the reservation may be punished if the sisters do not attend school. If you were Lucy, would you stay or would you leave? Explain why in a paragraph.

2. The girls' father says that leadership always comes with a price. What does he mean? Do you agree? Discuss this idea with a group of classmates. Use examples to support your view.

REVIEWING VOCABULARY

1. A person who is *forlorn* looks **(a)** sad **(b)** nervous **(c)** joyful.

2. You might find a *corset* in a **(a)** library **(b)** kitchen **(c)** clothes closet.

3. A *curtsy* is an old-fashioned gesture of **(a)** amusement **(b)** respect **(c)** affection.

4. People who are *quarantined* are **(a)** rewarded **(b)** questioned **(c)** isolated.

5. The school *infirmary* is used by students who are **(a)** disobedient **(b)** highly talented **(c)** ill.

6. When the teacher threatened to *switch* his pupils, he was giving a warning about **(a)** a punishment **(b)** a transfer to another school **(c)** a report.

7. Students of *elocution* usually practice **(a)** piano **(b)** gymnastics **(c)** public speaking.

8. A person who is *livid* feels **(a)** extremely shy **(b)** happy **(c)** angry.

THINKING CRITICALLY ABOUT CULTURE

1. In the play, what do you learn about the reasons for Lucy's unhappiness at school?

2. What do you learn about the customs and values of Native Americans?

3. What details in the play suggest that Lucy and Mother identify more with traditional Native American ways? What details show that Father and the other two girls value the learning of white people's ways?

4. How would you feel if you had to give up your roots or your cultural identity in order to "get ahead" by joining the "mainstream"?

5. Which of the characters do you think will hold on to Native American customs? Will each of the three sisters return to the reservation? Explain your answers.

WRITING PROJECTS

1. Assume that you are Father and that you are delivering a report to the tribal council about the events at the school. What issues will you mention to the tribe? Write the report that Father might give to the council.

2. Write an account of the play's events from the point of view of another Native American student or a white visitor. Remember that your understanding of events and your view of things are limited. For example, you will only know about the three sisters' inner feelings from what they say or do in the play.

Fighting for Freedom

Wiley M. Woodard

There is honor in fighting one's own battles. So imagine how you might feel if told you weren't good enough to fight for your own freedom.

Now, imagine that you get the chance to fight. The person next to you is doing the same job. But he is getting paid twice as much! Would you choose to risk your life in battle for half the pay that others get to do the same thing? This was the choice that free African Americans made in 1863.

Nearly 185,000 blacks fought for the Union Army during the Civil War. Sixteen of them won the nation's highest honor, the Congressional Medal of Honor. Nearly 40,000 gave their lives in the war.

In Fighting for Freedom, *we meet William and Aaron. They live in Massachusetts, the first state to recruit African Americans into the Union Army. These two free African Americans put up with low pay. They wear shabby uniforms. They face the hostility of white Union soldiers. Both are willing to fight for the day that all people in the United States will be free.*

VOCABULARY WORDS

seamstress (SEEM-strihs) a woman who is an expert at sewing
❖ The gown was made by a fine *seamstress*.

quota (KWOHT-uh) number that is allowed
❖ We filled our *quota* of three people for each car.

abolitionists (ab-uh-LIHSH-uhn-ihsts) people who wanted to end slavery
❖ Some African Americans were *abolitionists*.

snidely (SNEYD-lee) with sly sarcasm
❖ Some soldiers *snidely* mocked the officers.

bayonets (bay-uh-NEHTS) knives attached to rifles
❖ Soldiers used *bayonets* to stab their enemies.

parapet (PAHR-uh-Piht) protective wall in battle
❖ The troops took cover behind the fort's *parapet*.

KEY WORDS

Congressional Medal of Honor the nation's highest military award
❖ The *Congressional Medal of Honor* was first given in 1861.

Frederick Douglass African American writer and political activist
❖ *Frederick Douglass* escaped from slavery in 1838.

Union the states in the North that remained loyal to the United States in the Civil War
❖ Abraham Lincoln was President of the *Union*.

Confederacy the 11 states in the South that withdrew from the United States, causing the Civil War
❖ The states of the South withdrew from the Union and formed the *Confederacy*.

CHARACTERS

Aaron, William, and Marcus, *free African American men in their early twenties*
Colonel Robert Gould Shaw, *white commander of the Fifty-fourth Regiment*
Voice
White Officer
White Soldier 1
White Soldier 2
William H. Carney, *first African American winner of the Congressional Medal of Honor*

SETTING

Act One
Union recruitment station in Boston, Massachusetts

Act Two
Union training camp in Readville, Massachusetts

Act Three
Scene 1
Union training camp in Beaufort, South Carolina
Scene 2
Fort Wagner in South Carolina, July 18, 1863

Act Four
Army hospital

ACT ONE

Outside a Union Army recruitment station in Boston. It is morning, sometime after January 1863. Governor John Andrew of Massachusetts has given permission to recruit the first regiment of free African

Americans. This regiment will become the Fifty-fourth. A large crowd of black men have lined up. They are eagerly entering the recruiting station in hopes of joining this regiment. Aaron and William, two African American men and longtime friends, are standing outside the recruitment station viewing all the activity. Aaron is excited and enthusiastic about the Union war effort. William is calmer and less sure of his feelings about the war.

AARON: The only time I heard of this many excited black folks was when they announced an end to slavery in Boston.

WILLIAM: True. I expected a big turnout here this morning, but nothing like this.

AARON: It looks like every free black man of fighting age in Boston or roundabouts has come to join the Union Army.

(Marcus, Aaron's and William's friend, enters. He is talkative and has strong opinions.)

MARCUS: Morning.

WILLIAM: How you doing, Marcus?

MARCUS: Just fine. I was making a delivery for Miss Sadie, the seamstress, when I saw all these men lined up. What's all this fuss about?

WILLIAM: You mean you haven't heard any of the buzz around town or seen the recruiting posters? They've been up for weeks.

MARCUS: Well, let's hear your version of it.

WILLIAM: Well now, Governor Andrew is enlisting Negro troops in the Union Army. He's going to use Negroes to help fill the Massachusetts quota. These men want to join up. This regiment will be called the 54th Massachusetts Volunteers.

AARON: They're doing this across the North. I hear they got recruiting stations set up from here to St. Louis. A lot of black men may get the chance to fight.

MARCUS: Black men may get into the army, but they won't get to fight. The army only wants to use blacks to do the dirty work, so the white soldiers can be freed up to fight. They'll give black soldiers shovels, not rifles. *(Aaron and William look down a bit, disagreeing, but not wanting to argue.)* Believe me, the last thing that white soldiers want to see is a rifle in the hands of a black man.

AARON: *(in a serious voice)* Marcus, I reckon some of these men are volunteering because they want to work as laborers.

MARCUS: *(going on, as though briefly interrupted)* For the life of me, I don't understand why. Haven't we had enough of working for the white man? What would make a Negro want to volunteer to help win a white man's war?

WILLIAM: Maybe because these men feel the urge to do something to help our country. When this war began, we couldn't join up if we wanted to.

MARCUS: Our country? William, this country does not belong to you. You must be as simple as the rest of those men standing on that volunteer line. How can you feel any loyalty to a country that would bring Negroes here as slaves, and then treat us like it has? White people don't think Negroes will make good soldiers. Most think we don't have the courage to fight. These men standing on that line should go back home to their families, who need them.

WILLIAM: If that's so, then why did Congress pass a law that lets black men into the army?

MARCUS: So they could stop people like Frederick Douglass from bothering them about enlisting black troops. The Union Army can put up all the recruiting stations that it wants, but it doesn't want you.

AARON: These men who are volunteering have tasted freedom. Now they want to help end slavery in the South.

WILLIAM: Every day, a whole lot of slaves risk their lives to come north for freedom. A lot of them cross Union lines to join the army.

MARCUS: I know all about that. Somebody should tell them that this war is not about ending slavery. What President Lincoln really wants is to restore the Union. He said himself that this is a "white man's war."

WILLIAM: Well, I don't know . . . maybe Lincoln wants to end slavery and preserve the Union. He knows that not every white person supports slavery, Marcus. There are abolitionists fighting for our rights.

AARON: William is right. I hear that Governor Andrew is firmly against slavery. He's asked that Shaw fellow to lead this regiment.

MARCUS: Shaw who?

WILLIAM: Robert Gould Shaw. Shaw's from Massachusetts, and his parents are abolitionists. He's already seen two years of combat at places like Shiloh.

MARCUS: Hah! *(sarcastically)* That's very noble. *(pause)* I don't believe there's a white alive who has the best interests of blacks in mind. If white people do something to help Negroes, it's because they're getting something back.

AARON: Well, sir, I'll have you know, I'm thinking about joining the army myself. My family could really use the money the government will pay me if I enlist.

MARCUS: If I was you, I'd get my money up front because you might not get paid at all. Did the government ever pay slaves for the work they did? *(laughing to himself)* Besides, there is no guarantee that the slaves in the South will be freed by the government. I haven't heard any plans for that.

AARON: All I know is that I feel a storm of glory inside me when I picture myself marching in the Union Army. I think I'm going to join up. You still thinking about joining the Union army too, aren't you, William?

WILLIAM: Yes. You know I've been thinking about it for weeks. But you must admit that Marcus made some good points. Maybe we better consider this whole notion of joining just a little bit longer.

AARON: Consider what? I've made up my mind. I want to be part of this regiment. I want to fight to make sure my children stay free. I'm going to the recruiting station. You coming, William?

(Aaron heads towards the recruiting station.)

MARCUS: *(shaking his head as he watches Aaron)* You'd better take plenty of time to think about this, William.

(Aaron enters the recruiting station. After a moment's hesitation, William follows. Marcus looks sadly after him.)

ACT TWO, SCENE 1

A parade field at Readville, a flat, open area a few miles southwest of Boston. A group of African American recruits in ragged uniforms is being drilled in formation by a white officer in a Union uniform. One of the recruits is William. A group of white soldiers is watching from the edge of the field. They are also recruits, but their uniforms appear almost new. These soldiers are members of a new white regiment. As the black soldiers drill, the white soldiers mimic them. Two young white men, apparently farmers, are standing by themselves, taking in the entire scene.

OFFICER: About face! March! One, two, three—

(Voices of white soldiers are heard offstage, yelling at the recruits.)

FIRST SOLDIER: *(sarcastically)* Are you marching, or is that a dance you're doing?

SECOND SOLDIER: C'mon, fellas, you can dance better than that! Don't any of you boys play a banjo?

(laughter)

OFFICER: *(to the white soldiers)* You men report back to your barracks! Mind your own business!

FIRST SOLDIER: *(snidely)* You must be mighty proud, teaching a bunch of black boys to play soldier!

(more laughter, as the white soldiers walk away, their voices trailing off)

ACT TWO, SCENE 2

The training camp at Readville. The recruits are housed in large wooden barracks, seen in the foreground. Drilling grounds extend around the barracks. Most of the troops that make up the Fifty-fourth have been organized by Colonel Shaw into regiments of light and heavy artillery, cavalry, infantry, etc. Aaron and William are seated just outside the barracks, enjoying the evening air.

WILLIAM: Did you see that man who tried to skedaddle from the other camp last night? He was led back this morning with a bayonet at his rear.

AARON: I guess he had enough of this drilling.

WILLIAM: I can't say I haven't thought about running off myself. Drilling is dull business.

(pause)

AARON: *(distractedly)* Marcus was really dead-set against us joining up. I hope he looks in on our families from time to time like he promised.

WILLIAM: I miss my family so much. I knew it would be hard, but I didn't think I'd be missing them this much.

AARON: Me too. I pray for them every day, morning and evening.

WILLIAM: I miss my wife's smile. *(pause)* And I miss the smell of dinner cooking. I'd give anything for some cornpone, collard greens, side meat and gravy. . . .

AARON: *(suddenly more businesslike)* I'd give anything to get out of these rags. Do you think we'll ever get our dress blues?

WILLIAM: I don't know. I reckon. Can you believe they want to pay us only ten dollars a month? And three of those go for our clothes! I hear that white troops are getting thirteen dollars a month. And they get their uniforms free!

AARON: My family could really use that seven dollars, but I was proud of Shaw for turning it down. Unless they pay us the same as white soldiers, we shouldn't take any pay at all, I guess . . .

(There is silence between William and Aaron for a moment.)

AARON: *(continuing)* What're you thinking about?

WILLIAM: What happened today when I was out with the B company.

AARON: What was that?

WILLIAM: While we were being drilled by an officer who volunteered to help us, a company of white soldiers were yelling at us. They said some really ugly things. I heard some white soldiers say later that if they had to fight side-by-side with black troops, they would turn on us during battle.

AARON: That's bad, but not all white folks feel like that. Just the other day, a company of white soldiers called us "comrades in the struggle." And some of the white townsfolk came around here and told us that they were glad we'd have the chance to fight. They said Negroes should have the same rights as other citizens.

WILLIAM: Did you know that some of the officers tease Shaw about leading a Negro regiment? They call us children and tell him that the War Department

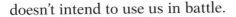

doesn't intend to use us in battle.

AARON: I know. But I heard Colonel Shaw tell those men that he is proud to lead this regiment.

WILLIAM: I hope he means that.

AARON: *(firmly)* I think he is saying it because he really means it.

ACT THREE, SCENE 1

The Union camp in Beaufort, South Carolina, near a clearing overlooking the ocean. Late evening in July 1863. The Fifty-fourth is assembled but at ease. Suddenly, a voice rises above the noise like a bullhorn.

VOICE: Silence in the ranks!

(Shaw enters. The men stand at attention.)

SHAW: *(in a dignified, sincere manner)* I've known for a long time that you men were ready for battle. I knew it way before we marched down to Battery Wharf and sailed south. I was proud of how warmly we've been greeted here in Beaufort. You men have become a first-class regiment. *(pause)* Now, some have said that no one will ever take Charleston without first silencing the forts that protect its harbor. If anybody will, I know the Fifty-fourth can.

(There is a murmur of agreement among the men.)

SOLDIER 1: We can do that!

SOLDIER 2: In no time!

SOLDIER 3: The Fifty-fourth can take Charleston!

SHAW: In order to do that, we must take Fort Wagner.

Fort Wagner is important because it guards every approach. I have asked the general to allow the Fifty-fourth to lead the attack.

(The soldiers cheer wildly.)

SHAW: *(continuing)* Once we get Fort Wagner, we can get past the guards at Fort Moultrie and Battery Gregg to take Fort Sumter. As you know, Fort Sumter is where this war started.

AARON: Then it's only right that the Fifty-fourth leads the attack.

(The soldiers chime in, all agreeing with Aaron.)

SHAW: You have served many months without pay. There were many who refused even to call you soldiers. Still, you pressed on with a faith that has brought you to this moment. You will soon bear arms in defense of freedom. You have answered the call to battle. I am glad to be among such brave men.

SOLDIER 1: We're ready, sir.

SHAW: I have no doubt, soldier. The other regiments have been formed. We will be moving you men out shortly.

(Shaw exits.)

AARON: How do you feel, William?

WILLIAM: A little nervous, to be honest.

AARON: Me too. But I'm excited at the same time.

WILLIAM: We'll be going into battle any time now.

AARON: It helps that we've seen a little action.

WILLIAM: But now we're leading in a major attack.

AARON: Look at it this way, William. Before long, we'll be back in Massachusetts. Maybe by Christmas. Think about all the stories we'll have to tell our families.

WILLIAM: I'll be so busy hugging and kissing everyone, I won't have time for telling stories.

AARON: Sure you will. You'll want to tell them all about how we took Fort Wagner. Tell them all about the brave Fifty-fourth.

WILLIAM: I can just hear you now, adding a little to the stories.

AARON: *(emphatically)* I'll tell them the truth. *(pause)* When this is over and we're back home, what's the first thing you're going to do?

WILLIAM: First thing I'll do is kiss my family to make up for all the time I was away. *(He smiles.)* What about you, Aaron?

AARON: First thing I'll do is eat a big plate of home-cooked food. I'm not joking! I've had enough of this army mush.

WILLIAM: *(a pause, and then seriously)* Good luck to you.

AARON: You too, William. And while you're fighting, just remember why we're here.

ACT THREE, SCENE 2

It is now dusk. Fort Wagner reaches across the narrow island from the ocean on the east to a marsh on the west. It is equipped with eleven heavy guns. A huge bombproof shelter has been constructed. We see only the staging area for the Union attack on Folly Island. Shaw stands behind the color bearer. Aaron is standing nearby.

SHAW: Officers to their posts. Fix bayonets! Charge bayonets! Fifty-fourth Massachusetts, forward march!

(The soldiers march quickly.)

SHAW: *(continuing)* Quick time, march!

(The soldiers pick up their pace and disappear, stage left.)

AARON: *(from offstage)* We have to keep together, men.

(We hear a bugle sound.)

SHAW: *(from offstage)* Double quick time—charge!

(The Fifty-fourth Massachusetts Volunteers race across a half-mile of sand toward the fort. They mount the parapet and struggle with the Confederate defenders. We hear the screams of battle offstage. It is clear that the charge is something of a suicide mission for the regiment. Soon the sky is ablaze with shells.)

ACT FOUR

It is now several weeks after the assault on Fort Wagner. In a small ward room in a private home converted into a makeshift troop hospital, William is lying in bed reading a book. He is heavily bandaged, still recovering from his wounds. William looks up from his book to greet his visitor, William H. Carney. Carney speaks formally, which indicates the official nature of his visit.

CARNEY: How you doing there, soldier?

WILLIAM: I'm coming along. I remember you, we served together—

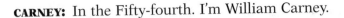

CARNEY: In the Fifty-fourth. I'm William Carney.

WILLIAM: My name is William, too. Aren't you the medal winner?

CARNEY: *(calmly)* Yes. Truth is, we all deserved that honor. Everybody is talking about the brave Fifty-fourth.

WILLIAM: With all those men falling around me, I thought the assault was a failure.

CARNEY: We lost many men. But it was the Fifty-fourth that made the first charge. With all that confusion, we didn't know where our reserve was.

WILLIAM: I don't remember what happened after I hit the ground.

CARNEY: I'll give you the story short, William. Our color bearer was killed on the parapet. Then Colonel Shaw grabbed the staff. A minute later, he fell himself. Soon the color staff was torn to pieces. Our white colonel was buried along with his black troops.

WILLIAM: *(softly)* Did all that dying really count for anything?

CARNEY: I'd say so. It meant a lot to me and every other member of the Fifty-fourth still living. It meant a lot to most of the white soldiers in the Union Army who have heard about it. And it meant a lot to the white folks who gave us the chance to prove ourselves. In fact, Congress has authorized President Lincoln to raise Negro troops on a large scale.

WILLIAM: *(in a strained voice, pushing himself up in bed)* I have been trying to get some information. Can you tell me what happened to my friend, Aaron?

CARNEY: He was one of the first to fall during the assault.

(William suppresses a sob.)

CARNEY: *(continuing)* Take heart, fellow. Aaron gave his life for a noble cause.

WILLIAM: What happens now?

CARNEY: There is talk of more assaults. The war, my friend, is not over. But your job here has ended. You've served your country well, and your mission is fulfilled. Go home to your family.

WILLIAM: I wonder if they'll believe what happened here. I did what I thought was right, but I wonder if I'd have had the courage without Aaron. I plan to tell his family that he was brave to the end. I hope that his folks, and all folks, will remember what happened at Fort Wagner.

READING FOR UNDERSTANDING

Act One

1. The Fifty-fourth Regiment was led by **(a)** Robert Shaw **(b)** William Carey **(c)** Aaron and Marcus.

2. Marcus's feelings about African American volunteers in the Civil War can best be described as **(a)** proud **(b)** eager **(c)** skeptical.

3. President Lincoln waged war against the South because he wanted to **(a)** restore the Union **(b)** free slaves in the South **(c)** help the economy.

Act Two

4. At first, African American soldiers in the Fifty-fourth Regiment were paid **(a)** more than white soldiers **(b)** less than white soldiers **(c)** the same as white soldiers.

5. Based on the play, you can assume that Colonel Shaw's attitude toward leading an all-African American regiment is **(a)** embarrassment **(b)** indifference **(c)** pride.

Act Three

6. Colonel Shaw prepared his men for an assault on **(a)** Fort Knox **(b)** Fort Apache **(c)** Fort Wagner.

7. At the end of Act Three, Scene 1, Aaron tells William to "remember why we're here." Aaron means that William should remember **(a)** the enslaved African Americans in the South **(b)** the hardships that his family is facing **(b)** what Marcus told them about prejudice.

Act Four

8. The final act takes place **(a)** on the battlefield **(b)** in a hospital **(c)** in Boston.

9. One result of the battle waged by the Fifty-fourth Regiment was that the Union Army began to **(a)** recruit African American troops in larger numbers **(b)** lose ground to the Confederate Army **(c)** recognize the contributions of Colonel Shaw.

RESPONDING TO THE PLAY

1. Why do you think that William and Aaron made the sacrifices they did? Why do you think Marcus felt the way he did? Explain your answer.

2. Choose one event or statement in the play that made a strong impression on you. Then explain how that event or statement affected you.

REVIEWING VOCABULARY

The following sentences are about the play. Decide which of the following words best fits each blank. Write your answers on a separate sheet of paper.

1. Colonel Shaw ordered the troops to fix their _____ to the end of their rifles.

2. Miss Sadie was a _____, a woman who is an expert at sewing.

3. Governor Andrew used Negro troops to fill the Massachusetts _____ in the Union Army.

4. In launching their attack, the Fifty-fourth Regiment mounted the _____ that had protected them from enemy fire.

5. Lincoln knew that the _____ supported an end to slavery.

6. The officer did not hear the soldier who _____ mocked him.

Words: *parapet, seamstress, snidely, quota, bayonets, abolitionists*

THINKING CRITICALLY

1. What does Marcus predict about racism in the army?
2. Is Marcus's prediction right? How does racism affect William and Aaron?
3. Describe a time when you or someone you know was a victim of prejudice. How did it feel? How did it change your views about people?
4. In the late 1940s, President Harry S. Truman desegregated the U.S. Armed Forces. Why do you think it took so long?

WRITING PROJECTS

1. Assume that you are William. Write a letter to Aaron's family about how he died bravely in action. Discuss what his friendship meant to you.
2. The playwright describes the battle at Fort Wagner. Pick a movie or TV battle that you've seen. In one paragraph, describe the scene. Use action words to make the scene come alive.

The Trial of Sacco and Vanzetti

Rafaela Ellis

From 1918 to 1922, the United States faced two big problems. Millions of people had no jobs. Wages were low. Workers called strikes. Many striking workers were new to this country. Some Americans thought these immigrants were a danger to the government.

Nicola Sacco and Bartolomeo Vanzetti were two Italian immigrant workers. In 1921, they were tried for murder. They were found guilty and put to death. This play is based on their trial.

Sacco and Vanzetti had radical ideas about government. Some people feared these ideas. They wanted the men punished, whether they were guilty of committing the crime or not.

Were Sacco and Vanzetti on trial for murder? Or were they on trial for their beliefs? Read the play and decide.

VOCABULARY WORDS

anarchists (AN-uhr-kihsts) people against all forms of government
- ❖ The government feared that *anarchists* would blow up the building.

verdict (VER-dihkt) decision of a jury
- ❖ The courtroom grew quiet when the jury gave its *verdict*.

appeal (uh-PEEL) a request to have a case reviewed by a higher court
- ❖ The lawyer was sure an *appeal* would be granted.

alibi (AL-uh-by) statement that proves that a person accused of a crime could not have committed the crime
- ❖ The bus driver supported the defendant's *alibi* that he was on the bus.

clemency (KLEM-uhn-see) mercy; forgiveness
- ❖ The criminal begged the judge for *clemency*.

radicals (RAD-ih-kuhlz) people who want big changes in government
- ❖ The British thought the colonists were *radicals*.

CHARACTERS

Courtney Watchman, *a reporter for the* Bean Town Bugle
Mr. Waverly Flagg, *an opponent of Sacco and Vanzetti*
Mrs. Truly Freeman, *a supporter of Sacco and Vanzetti*
Whit Nesser, *a court reporter*
Frederick G. Katzmann, *the prosecuting attorney*
Michael J. Connolly, *the arresting officer*
Webster Thayer, *the presiding judge*
Fred H. Moore, *the attorney for the defense*
Nicola Sacco, *a shoemaker on trial for murder*
Bartolomeo Vanzetti, *a fish peddler and Sacco's codefendant*
Celestino Madeiros, *a convicted murderer*
Rosina Sacco, *Sacco's wife*

SETTING

Act One
Scene 1
Near the Dedham, Massachusetts courthouse steps, summer of 1921

Scene 2
Inside the courtroom

Scene 3
Outside the courthouse

Act Two
Scene 1
Sacco's jail cell in the Dedham Jail, 1925

Scene 2
A visiting area of the Charlestown State Prison, 1927

Scene 3
Sacco's jail cell

ACT ONE, SCENE 1

***W**atchman stands in a phone booth* near the steps of the Dedham courthouse. *Around her, the shouts of a large crowd can be heard.*

WATCHMAN: *(shouting into phone)* Boss? Yeah, it's Watchman. I'm outside the courthouse in Dedham. In Massachusetts. *(pause)* What? I can't hear you. The crowd is too loud. There must be five thousand people out here. *(pause)* What do you mean, "What's going on?" It's the case of the century, boss. Haven't you heard? Yeah, the Sacco and Vanzetti case—the Italian immigrants charged with stealing sixteen thousand dollars from a shoe factory and gunning down two guards. *(pause)* The protestors? They think these guys have been framed. Yeah. Well, for one thing, they're immigrants. Immigrants are very unpopular these days. And everyone says they're anarchists. *(pause)* Anarchists. People who don't believe in any form of government. *(pause)* A-N-A-R . . . Oh, look it up in the dictionary! *(pause)* I don't know what to think, boss. I'll have to hear the facts at the trial. *(pause)* Yeah. It's just about to start. I'll let you know. Goodbye.

(Watchman hangs up the phone and walks through the crowd to the courthouse entrance. As she tries to enter the courthouse, a man with a sign reading "GUILTY!" stops her.)

FLAGG: You're a reporter, aren't you?

WATCHMAN: I'm Courtney Watchman, *Bean Town Bugle.*

FLAGG: Well, I'm Waverly Flagg, president of the group

America for Americans. I have something to say.

WATCHMAN: Look, I have to get into the courtroom. The trial is starting.

FLAGG: Sure. The press never wants to listen to a real American. You're too busy telling people that these guys didn't do it. They did! They're as guilty as sin.

WATCHMAN: How can you be sure?

FLAGG: Look around, lady. The United States is in trouble. Do you know how many outsiders we've let into the country in the past twenty years? Italians, Poles, Slavs. They're everywhere. And what do they bring to this, the best country in the world? Anarchy. Communism. Look at this Sacco and Vanzetti. They should thank their lucky stars that they live in this great land. But what do they do? They talk about anarchy. They want to overthrow the government. They say we should have no government at all. And then they gun down innocent men! I say we should throw the book at them! I think . . .

(A woman from the crowd rushes in and interrupts Watchman and Flagg.)

FREEMAN: You're not actually listening to this man, are you? Bigotry! Prejudice! That's what he's all about. If you want the truth, talk to me.

WATCHMAN: And you are. . . ?

FREEMAN: I'm Truly Freeman of the American Civil Rights Society.

FLAGG: Another bleeding heart!

WATCHMAN: *(looking at Mrs. Freeman)* So, you don't think Sacco and Vanzetti killed the guards?

FREEMAN: Of course not. Where's the proof? The police arrested them because their car looked like the killers' car. Do you know how many dark Buicks there are in Boston? Even the judge has called Sacco and Vanzetti "rotten anarchists." That just proves these men are on trial for their politics. Ever since the government of Russia was overthrown four years ago, Americans have been afraid of anyone who talks about politics. Afraid someone is going to overthrow *our* government. And, of course, people like him *(pointing to Flagg)* think every immigrant is a criminal. It's just a shame. The whole world is laughing at us. And we call this country a democracy!

WATCHMAN: Yeah . . . Well look, I've got to get into court. Thanks for talking to me. Both of you. *(Watchman walks toward the entrance, then turns and looks back at the crowd.)* I don't know what to believe.

ACT ONE, SCENE 2

Inside the courtroom. Sacco and Vanzetti, dressed in suits, sit at the defense table along with their lawyer, Fred Moore. On the witness stand sits Officer Connolly, who is being questioned by the prosecutor, Frederick Katzmann. Watchman enters quietly and takes a seat in the back of the courtroom, next to reporter Whit Nesser.

WATCHMAN: Hey, Whit. What did I miss?

NESSER: You're just in time for the good part.

KATZMANN: And why did you arrest these two men?

CONNOLLY: They went to Johnson's Garage to pick up a dark car, a Buick, like the one used in the murders.

We told Mr. Johnson to call us if any Italians came for that car. When they did, we arrested them.

KATZMANN: And Mr. Benjamin Bowles picked them out as the men who killed the payroll guards?

CONNOLLY: He picked out the one with the moustache.

KATZMANN: That would be Vanzetti.

CONNOLLY: Yeah, that's the one.

KATZMANN: And what did you find, officer, when you searched Sacco and Vanzetti?

CONNOLLY: They both had guns. Vanzetti, he had a thirty-eight caliber revolver, fully loaded. The little guy, Sacco, had bullets in his pocket and a thirty-two caliber Colt pistol.

KATZMANN: And do you know, officer, what type of gun was used to shoot the shoe company guards?

CONNOLLY: A thirty-two caliber Colt.

(The courtroom erupts in noise.)

THAYER: Order! Order in this court! *(quietly to Katzmann)* Good going, Katzmann. I think we've got them now!

KATZMANN: No more questions.

MOORE: No questions, your honor.

KATZMANN: The prosecution rests.

THAYER: Mr. Moore, are you going to present a defense?

MOORE: Of course, your honor.

THAYER: I was afraid of that. Go ahead, then.

MOORE: The defense calls Nicola Sacco.

(Sacco, looking scared, rises and walks slowly to the stand.)

THAYER: Raise your hand, Sacco. Do you swear to tell the truth, the whole truth, and nothing but the truth?

SACCO: I swear.

THAYER: Sit down.

MOORE: Mr. Sacco, were you carrying a gun on the night of May 5th, 1920?

SACCO: Yes, sir.

MOORE: Why?

SACCO: I was scared.

MOORE: Of whom?

SACCO: Police.

MOORE: Why were you scared of the police, Mr. Sacco?

SACCO: They killed Salsedo.

KATZMANN: Objection, your honor! The police are not on trial here!

MOORE: Please, your honor. I'm trying to show why the man had a gun.

THAYER: Be careful, Mr. Moore.

MOORE: Yes, your honor. Mr. Sacco, what do you mean, "They killed Salsedo."

SACCO: Salsedo, my friend. He was in the group. The anarchy group . . .

KATZMANN: He admits that he's an anarchist!

MOORE: *(He gives Katzmann an angry look, then turns to Sacco.)* And you believe the police killed Mr. Salsedo?

SACCO: Salsedo, he stand on the street and give people—what do you call?—pamphlets. About the government. The police don't like that. They take him to the station. They beat him. Me and Bart . . .

MOORE: You mean, Mr. Vanzetti.

SACCO: Yes, Bartolomeo. Me and Bart, we find Salsedo dead on the street. That's why we get guns. That's why we try to get the car.

MOORE: Why did you need the car?

SACCO: We want to drive to river. To dump pamphlets. So we don't end up like Salsedo.

MOORE: Mr. Sacco, did you rob the Slater and Morrill Shoe Factory and kill two guards?

SACCO: I never hurt anybody. Me, I make shoes. I like the shoe factory!

MOORE: That's all, Mr. Sacco. Thank you. *(Moore returns to his seat.)*

THAYER: Your witness, Mr. Katzmann.

KATZMANN: *(He walks toward the witness stand.)* Are you an anarchist, Sacco?

SACCO: I don't know.

KATZMANN: You don't know? You just said you had anarchist pamphlets!

SACCO: I think about things. I'm not sure what right, what wrong. I just think about things. Maybe something be better for people, for working people. I go to a group. We talk about things . . . about people.

KATZMANN: Sounds like an anarchist to me!

MOORE: I object, your honor!

KATZMANN: Forget it. I'm done with Mr. Sacco.

THAYER: You can step down, Sacco.

(Sacco leaves the stand and returns to his seat.)

MOORE: I call Bartolomeo Vanzetti to the stand.

(Vanzetti rises, walks to the bench, and raises his hand. Although nothing is spoken, the movement shows that Judge Thayer is swearing him in. Vanzetti sits in the witness chair.)

MOORE: Mr. Vanzetti, I'll come right to the point. Did you kill the shoe company guards?

VANZETTI: No, sir, I did not.

MOORE: Why did you have a gun on the night of May 5th?

VANZETTI: Like Nick said . . . to protect us from the police.

MOORE: Have you ever robbed or killed anyone, Mr. Vanzetti?

VANZETTI: No. I've never done anything like that.

MOORE: No further questions. *(Moore returns to his seat.)*

THAYER: Questions, Mr. Katzmann?

KATZMANN: Oh, yes. *(He walks towards Vanzetti.)* Are you an American citizen, Vanzetti?

VANZETTI: Yes, sir.

KATZMANN: And how old are you?

VANZETTI: Thirty-three years.

KATZMANN: So, I guess you served in the war, then—in the World War, from 1917 to 1919.

VANZETTI: No.

KATZMANN: No? A strong, healthy man like you? Why not?

VANZETTI: I . . . I was in Mexico.

KATZMANN: Why did you go to Mexico? So you wouldn't have to serve in the war?

VANZETTI: No, I . . . I mean, yes. I don't believe in war.

KATZMANN: *(angrily)* You don't believe in defending the United States of America?

VANZETTI: No, no! I don't believe in any war. Enough war in the world already. We don't need any more war!

KATZMANN: So, you're a draft dodger! Are you an anarchist, too, Vanzetti?

(Vanzetti is silent.)

KATZMANN: I asked you a question, Vanzetti! Are you an anarchist?

VANZETTI: I . . . I believe . . . Yes! I am an anarchist. Government is bad for people. Government . . .

KATZMANN: Government what? Should be overthrown?

VANZETTI: I don't know. I just know that it doesn't work right.

KATZMANN: You're a no-good, rotten anarchist! A draft dodger and an anarchist! No further questions!

(Vanzetti looks helplessly at his lawyer, and leaves the stand. As the lawyers move silently in the background, making their closing statements. Nesser and Watchman begin to whisper to one another.)

NESSER: What do you think, Miss *Bean Town Bugle*?

WATCHMAN: I don't know what to think. How about you?

NESSER: Well, some of the evidence is strong: a similar car, a similar gun. But they didn't prove it was the same car or the same gun.

WATCHMAN: And they never said what happened to the money. But that draft dodger stuff is going to hurt. And Vanzetti's views about government—that scares people. It's bound to affect the jury.

NESSER: You're right. I think both these guys are in a lot of trouble.

ACT ONE, SCENE 3

Outside the courthouse. Watchman fights her way toward the courthouse door through a loud and angry crowd. Groups are pushing and shoving one another. As Watchman reaches the door, she runs into Nesser, who is coming out of the courthouse.

NESSER: You missed it, Court.

WATCHMAN: Did the jury reach a verdict?

NESSER: They did. Didn't take them long.

WATCHMAN: And. . . ?

NESSER: What do you think? Guilty.

WATCHMAN: I should have known by the way this crowd is acting.

NESSER: Look! Here come Thayer and Katzmann.

(Judge Thayer and Mr. Katzmann are seen shaking hands and smiling. The crowd begins to boo. Watchman, pen and pad in hand, walks up to the judge.)

WATCHMAN: Judge Thayer, you seem happy with the jury's verdict.

THAYER: Justice was served, ma'am. We can't have these dirty anarchists running around in our streets, causing trouble. *(turning to Katzmann)* Isn't that right, Mr. Prosecutor? Yes, it was a fine verdict. It will teach these foreign radicals to watch their step!

(Thayer and Katzmann walk away, smiling. Sacco and Vanzetti, in handcuffs, are led out of the courthouse by police officers. Their lawyer walks out behind them.)

CROWD: FREE SACCO AND VANZETTI! FREE SACCO AND VANZETTI!

WATCHMAN: Mr. Sacco! Mr. Vanzetti! What do you have to say?

SACCO: We didn't kill nobody.

VANZETTI: We're innocent!

WATCHMAN: Mr. Moore, do you plan an appeal?

MOORE: Oh, yes, we'll appeal. We won't stop until these innocent men are free. *(turning to the crowd)* We won't stop! We'll NEVER stop! Free Sacco and Vanzetti!

CROWD: FREE SACCO AND VANZETTI! FREE SACCO

AND VANZETTI! FREE SACCO AND VANZETTI!

(As the crowd chants, the police drag Sacco and Vanzetti off to jail.)

ACT TWO, SCENE 1

Sacco's jail cell in the Dedham Jail, 1925. Sacco, Vanzetti, and Fred Moore are seated in Sacco's jail cell. A police officer stands guard just outside the cell.

MOORE: That reporter, Miss Watchman of the *Bugle*, is on her way in. Before she gets here, I wanted to tell you about our latest appeal.

VANZETTI: Judge Thayer, he said no. He rejected the appeal, right?

MOORE: Yes, he turned us down. But don't worry— we're not giving up.

SACCO: Not giving up. Not giving up! You say this for five years. And for five years, we sit in jail. My wife and my son, they are all alone. For five years!

VANZETTI: Three appeals! Every time, the judge say no. First, we prove the jury foreman told everybody he hates Italians. The judge say no appeal. Then we show Katzmann covered up an alibi witness. Again, the judge say no. Now we find out the police maybe lied about the bullets. They said Sacco's bullets matched the killers', but they can't prove it. Still, the judge say no. No matter what we do, all Judge Thayer say is no, no, no!

(Watchman arrives at the cell door, and the police guard lets her in.)

MOORE: Hello, Miss Watchman.

WATCHMAN: Hello, Mr. Moore. *(turning to Sacco and Vanzetti)* Hello, Mr. Sacco, Mr. Vanzetti. I heard about what happened in court. Maybe these will cheer you up. *(She pulls out a stack of letters.)*

VANZETTI: Letters?

WATCHMAN: From all over the world. And from some of the most important people in the country. They've been writing to the *Bugle* every day. They want the state to set you free.

SACCO: Important people care about two poor men like us?

WATCHMAN: They do. Look, this one's from Upton Sinclair, the award-winning novelist. And here's a letter from Katherine Anne Porter, the short-story writer. Oh, and we just got some news at the office. The poet Edna St. Vincent Millay was arrested for protesting your prison stay.

MOORE: That kind of support can't hurt. But we still need some new evidence to file another appeal.

(Suddenly, loud yelling is heard outside the cell. The guard rushes from the door and heads down the hall. The yelling becomes louder and gets closer.)

MADEIROS: I wanna talk to that lawyer! I got something to say!

(The guard brings Madeiros to the door of Sacco's cell.)

MADEIROS: Are you Moore, the lawyer?

MOORE: Yes.

MADEIROS: *(rudely)* Yeah. You look like a lawyer.

MOORE: And who are you?

MADEIROS: I'm Celestino Madeiros. I got something to tell you.

MOORE: I'm listening.

MADEIROS: These guys didn't kill the payroll clerks.

MOORE: I know that. But do you know who did?

MADEIROS: Yeah, I know who did. *(proudly)* I did. Me and the Morelli gang.

MOORE: The Morelli gang? That band of thugs from Providence, Rhode Island?

MADEIROS: Yeah. We've done a lot of holdups. This one kinda got out of hand. We didn't really want to kill those guards, but they wouldn't give up the loot. What a couple of patsies! Anyway, I'm in here for murder already. So I figure, why let these guys take my rap?

MOORE: Mr. Madeiros, would you be willing to testify in court? To say, before a judge, that you killed the payroll clerks?

MADEIROS: Aren't you listening, pal? No wonder these guys are still in jail! Yeah, I'll testify. What have I got to lose?

MOORE: This is the break we've been waiting for! I'll file the papers immediately. *(Moore rushes out, as the guard takes Madeiros away.)*

WATCHMAN: This is the break I've been waiting for! Whit Nesser has never had a scoop like this. *(Watchman rushes out.)*

SACCO: Bart, you think maybe this time, the judge say yes?

VANZETTI: After all these years, Nick, I am afraid to

hope. So many years. So many lost hopes. But who knows? Maybe this time, the judge say yes. *(The two men smile, then hug each other. The guard returns and takes Vanzetti back to his cell. Sacco takes a photo from the wall of his cell and looks at it.)*

SACCO: Ah, Rosina, my dear wife. You wait so long. Maybe your wait is over. Maybe this time, the judge say yes.

ACT TWO, SCENE 2

A visiting area of the Charlestown State Prison, 1927. Sacco, Vanzetti, and Moore walk slowly into the room. All the men are wearing suits and coats. As they enter, they begin removing their hats. It is clear they have just returned from somewhere. After they enter the room, they are silent for a long while. Then, Fred Moore speaks.

MOORE: I don't know what to say to you men. I know we should have seen this coming. Everyone said we should expect it. But I didn't. I didn't believe they'd do it. I'm so sorry . . .

SACCO: It's okay, Fred. You did all you could.

VANZETTI: We don't blame you, Fred.

MOORE: I mean, we thought Judge Thayer would turn down the Madeiros appeal. He hates us. He's never tried to hide it. But then the state's Supreme Judicial Court denied the appeal, too. And now, Judge Thayer has imposed that sentence . . .

VANZETTI: The maximum sentence . . .

SACCO: Death.

(The men are silent for a long moment. Then a guard

comes to the door with Watchman.)

WATCHMAN: I had to come.

MOORE: Yes, I'm sure Judge Thayer's sentence will be front-page news.

WATCHMAN: It's more than just that. It's what has happened since.

MOORE: What do you mean?

WATCHMAN: We're getting reports from all over the world. Protests have broken out in New York, London, all over the place. The police in Boston are on high alert. Everyone is outraged by this sentence!

SACCO: Not everyone. Judge Thayer, he knows a lot of people don't like us. A lot of people think we're just rotten foreigners.

VANZETTI: Two Italians who want to overthrow the government.

MOORE: That's why people are protesting. Don't you see? Many people think that the sentence, the whole case, is about prejudice. Prejudice against who you are and what you believe.

WATCHMAN: So what's your next step, Fred?

MOORE: We'll ask Governor Fuller for clemency.

SACCO: Clemency?

MOORE: It means we'll ask the governor of Massachusetts to overrule the judge. To say that you and Bart should not get the death penalty.

VANZETTI: The governor can do that?

MOORE: Yes. The governor has that power.

VANZETTI: But will he use it? That's the question now.

WATCHMAN: It's possible, Mr. Vanzetti. Governor Fuller is under a lot of pressure. And it's not just the protests. A lot of powerful people—famous, wealthy people—are behind you.

VANZETTI: Thank you, Miss Watchman. You've been very kind. But let's face it. A lot of famous, wealthy people are against us, too. The mood in the country is bad right now. People are afraid. We're foreigners. Radicals. For some people, that's enough.

SACCO: Enough to put us to death.

MOORE: Bart, Nick . . . please don't give up hope now. You've got to be strong. There's still a chance. We have to believe there's still a chance.

(In the background, the faint noise of a chanting crowd begins to be heard. No one seems to notice it at first.)

SACCO: Fred, you're a good man. We so grateful for all you have done for us. But after six years, hope is not so easy. You tell us to hope. But we knew from the start. We always knew it would come to this.

(The crowd noise has become louder now, and the room is still as Sacco, Vanzetti, Moore, and Watchman listen.)

WATCHMAN: It was only a matter of time.

SACCO: What is it?

WATCHMAN: Your supporters. They've come to the jail. They want you to know that they're not giving up.

MOORE: You see, men? They're not giving up. Now, don't you give up!

(Sacco and Vanzetti look at one another and shake

their heads. The chanting outside the jail is getting louder now, and we can hear the cry: "SAVE SACCO AND VANZETTI!")

VANZETTI: What friends we have, Nick! For six years, Fred has worked to free us. Now, these people come. Listen to them! Thousands of people we've never known. Coming here to tell us not to give up.

SACCO: Okay, Fred. Write your letter to the governor. One more time, we'll try to hope.

(Moore walks over and shakes Vanzetti's hand, then Sacco's. The three men stand together, as Watchman looks on, smiling.)

ACT TWO, SCENE 3

Sacco's jail cell at the Charlestown Prison, 1927. Sacco and his wife sit on Sacco's cot, holding hands. In the far corner of the room, Vanzetti and Moore are seen talking quietly. Occasionally, Vanzetti and Moore look over at the Saccos, shake their heads, and look away. The spotlight shines on Sacco and his wife.

SACCO: My dear Rosina. You've been so strong. But you must be stronger. You must not break. We have a son. He will never know his father. You must be strong for him. You will be his only strength.

ROSINA: Don't say that, Nick. There still time. The governor, he could call. The paper say the governor maybe change his mind.

SACCO: Rosina, it's too late! The governor, he put together a panel. All big men in this group—a judge and two college presidents. The president of the Harvard University! They talk and talk. All to decide if we should live or die. And they said we should die. It's too late.

ROSINA: *(crying)* Nicola, Nicola. What will I do? What will become of us?

SACCO: Ah, my Rosina.

(Sacco and his wife hug. The spotlight shifts to the corner of the room, where Vanzetti and Moore are talking.)

MOORE: You know, Bart, that we'll do all we can for your families. A lot of people have raised money.

VANZETTI: I don't think Mrs. Sacco is worried about money, Fred.

MOORE: I know. I'm sorry, Bart. I just don't know what to say any more.

VANZETTI: *(laughing softly)* My poor Fred! You've been talking about us for six years. Now you've run out of words! It's okay, my friend. We know you did all you could. *(He looks at the Saccos and shakes his head.)* It's easier for me. My sister, she's all the family I have. She cried today when she came, the last time she'll see me. But it's not the same. Rosina and Nick, they have so much love. They've suffered so much. You know, Rosina still thinks the governor will call. Nick, he tells her it won't happen. But she keeps saying, "He will call. He will call."

MOORE: I wish he would, Bart. I wish to heaven he would.

VANZETTI: Fred, you still don't want to give up, do you? You still have that look in your eye. You think you can change things, even now.

MOORE: I'm not giving up, Bart. Even if you and Nick

. . . even if the governor doesn't call, I won't give up. I'll fight to clear your names. I won't let you go down in history as a murderer, Bart. I won't.

(A guard brings Courtney Watchman to the door of the jail cell. Moore looks up and nods at the guard, and he lets Watchman enter. She is dressed somberly in black. As she enters, everyone looks up at her.)

WATCHMAN: I'm sorry to intrude, gentlemen. Oh, Mrs. Sacco, I'm sorry. I didn't know you were here.

SACCO: It's all right, Miss Watchman. Rosina knows you are a friend.

WATCHMAN: I feel terrible asking this. I feel awful even being here. But my editor wants to know . . .

VANZETTI: If we have any last words.

WATCHMAN: Yes. If there is anything you want to say.

VANZETTI: *(taking a piece of paper from his coat pocket)* I have thought about this. I have thought, "What do I want to say? What do I want people to know about us?" These are not my last words, Miss Watchman. My last words, my last thoughts, will be for my family and friends. But this is what I want people to know. *(looking at the paper, then looking up)* First, about Nick. I am a better talker than he is, but he is a better man. Many times, I have felt small seeing how brave he is. How he has suffered for nothing. As for me, I have suffered for things I am not guilty of. I have suffered because I am Italian. And indeed, I am Italian. I have suffered because I am a radical. And indeed, I am a radical. But if I had my life to live over again, I would do what I have already done. This case make people think. About prejudice. About what is right, and what is wrong. Those crowds outside, they're thinking. If it had not been for this case, I might have live out my life an unknown, a failure. Now, we are not a failure. This is our triumph. Never in our life can we hope to do such work for tolerance, for justice, for man's understanding of man, as we do now by accident. Our words, our lives, our pains—nothing! The taking of our lives—the lives of a good shoemaker and a poor fish peddler—all! This last agony is our triumph! *(He puts the paper away.)* Tell your editor, this is what Vanzetti said.

(The room is still. Then a guard comes to the door. Moore looks up, nods, and then walks slowly to the two men.)

MOORE: It's time, men.

ROSINA: No! No, please!

SACCO: Remember, Rosina. You must be strong.

(Sacco and Rosina hug. Sacco and Vanzetti each hug Moore and nod at Watchman. Then they walk out of the cell, with Rosina behind them. Watchman and Moore watch them go, then stand silently for a moment. At last, Moore speaks.)

MOORE: So, Miss Watchman, what will it say in tomorrow's *Bean Town Bugle?*

WATCHMAN: Just this: that today, August 23, 1927, Sacco and Vanzetti were executed for murder. We may never know what really happened the night the shoe company was robbed and the two guards were killed. We may never know who really committed that crime, or why. But we know that Sacco and Vanzetti were tried for more than murder. They were tried because they were immigrants, and people are afraid of immigrants. They were tried because they were radicals, and people are afraid of radicals. And, in the end, they paid the ultimate price for who they were and for what they believed. That's what I'll say in tomorrow's paper, Fred. Because that's what I believe.

READING FOR UNDERSTANDING

Overview

1. Put these incidents in the correct order.
   (a) Judge Thayer hands down the death sentence.
   (b) Madeiros claims that he committed the crime.
   (c) The Supreme Judicial Court turns down Moore's request for an appeal.
   (d) Moore asks the governor of Massachusetts for clemency.
   (e) Judge Thayer turns down a request for an appeal.

Act One

2. Why did people want Sacco and Vanzetti convicted?
3. According to the police officer, what is the evidence against them? How do the two men explain the car and guns?
4. Why didn't Vanzetti serve in World War I? Why does the prosecutor want the jury to know that?

Act Two

5. Why do you think Madeiros's testimony did not change the outcome of the play?
6. Why do Fred Moore and Courtney Watchman feel that the governor will grant clemency?
7. How long have the two men been in prison?
8. How does Vanzetti explain to people that his death is a triumph?

RESPONDING TO THE PLAY

1. Reread the speech that Vanzetti makes near the end of the play. He says that his life has not been a failure. He made people think about prejudice. Do you think that most people in his shoes would feel the same way? Describe your thoughts in a paragraph.

2. The case of Sacco and Vanzetti is about prejudice and justice. Do you know of another time when prejudice stopped justice? Write a paragraph describing the incident.

REVIEWING VOCABULARY

Match each word on the left with the correct definition on the right.

1. clemency
2. radicals
3. alibi
4. anarchists
5. verdict
6. appeal

a. people against all governments
b. request to have a case reviewed
c. decision made by a jury
d. people who want big changes in government
e. mercy or forgiveness
f. statement proving that a person accused of a crime could not have committed the crime

THINKING CRITICALLY

1. Why did people fear Sacco and Vanzetti? Can it ever be wrong for people to express their ideas? Explain your answer.

2. How were fears of radical ideas related to feelings about immigrants?

3. What do you think of Madeiros's confession? Why might he confess to a crime that he didn't commit?

4. Should a judge allow a prosecutor to question someone's political beliefs? Why or why not?

5. When Vanzetti talks about his execution, he says, "This last agony is our triumph!" What does he mean?

6. Sacco and Vanzetti were anarchists because they believed government didn't work. Do you think society could work without a strong government?

WRITING PROJECT

Write a short, one-act courtroom drama based on a social or political issue. You may, for example, have read about environmentalists who tried to stop developers from cutting down trees. Or write about animal rights activists who tried to shut down laboratories that used animals for research. Look through newspapers and magazines for other examples.

In your play, write dialogue that shows what the character on trial believes. Also include the arguments that the defending and the prosecuting lawyers use. Be sure to state the decision that the jury reaches.

Dust Bowl Journey

Carroll Moulton

The Great Depression was a terrible time for people all around the world. It began in 1929, with an economic collapse that led to misery for millions of people. Companies went out of business. Banks failed. Millions of people lost their houses and jobs.

Also, in the United States in the 1930s, low rainfall and overplanting of crops turned the Great Plains into a "Dust Bowl." Strong winds blew the topsoil away. Farmers could no longer grow crops in the Dust Bowl.

Thousands of families left their farms. They headed to California in search of work. Many were from Oklahoma. Some Californians resented the newcomers and called them "Okies." The Depression hit hard in California as well. The arrival of farmers from the Great Plains meant competition for few jobs.

The violence that the Bergman family of Dust Bowl Journey meets on its journey was common. Admire the courage they showed in the face of hardship.

VOCABULARY WORDS

robust (roh-BUST) sturdy, appearing to be in vigorous health
- ❖ Years of exercise made him strong and *robust*.

saplings (SAP-lihngz) young trees
- ❖ The *saplings* that we planted are now the tallest trees in the village.

makeshift (MAYK-shihft) a temporary and often poorly made substitute
- ❖ Migrant workers often lived in *makeshift* shelters.

rattletrap (RAT-ul-trap) rickety; ready to fall apart
- ❖ Farmers hoped their *rattletrap* vehicles would not break down.

pawnbroker (PAWN-brohk-uhr) a person who lends money for personal property left as security
- ❖ To get money to pay our rent, we left our jewelry with a *pawnbroker*.

KEY WORD

Route 66 a major east-west highway used for travel from the Midwest to California during the 1930s
- ❖ *Route 66* is no longer a popular highway for drivers traveling west.

CHARACTERS

Kirsten Bergman, *mother*
Helga Ulfung, *the Bergman family's neighbor*
Nils Bergman, *father*
Tom Bergman, *son, age sixteen*
Karen Bergman, *daughter, age fifteen*
Jeeter, *bully*
Harris, *bully*
Two other bullies
Sammy Nakasone, *agent of the Farm Security
    Administration*

SETTING

Act One

The interior of the Bergman farmhouse near Holcomb,
Kansas, late afternoon, November 10, 1933

Act Two

The same, six months later

Act Three

Somewhere on Route 66, just outside Barstow,
California, late June 1934

Act Four

A migrant labor camp on the outskirts of San
Bernardino, California, late afternoon

ACT ONE

*I**nterior of the Bergman farmhouse**
near Holcomb, Kansas. Late afternoon,
November 10, 1933. We see Kirsten
Bergman, robust and blond, busily making
dinner before the return of her husband Nils
and her two children, Tom and Karen. Helga Ulfung, a*

neighbor, keeps Kirsten company in the kitchen.

KIRSTEN: Did you say it was nearly five o'clock, Helga?

HELGA: It's about ten minutes past.

KIRSTEN: Oh my, and nearly dark, too. I should have put on the biscuits by this time. Nils is always home by five-thirty, and I've never known that man to wait for his supper.

(She opens the oven door and neatly places a tray on the middle shelf.)

HELGA: My Axel doesn't think we can make it one more year, Kirsten, what with wheat prices the way they are. How're you and Nils riding things out?

KIRSTEN: Oh, Helga, it's going to be hard. Why just the other day I had to pay five dollars on the bill at the grocery store. Mr. Andersen down at the bank said we could go one more month without a payment on the equipment loan, but then . . . I know one thing for sure, though. Nils will never leave this farm. If someone can make a go of the farm, I know Nils will. I'd better put the lights on.

(She busies herself lighting the kerosene lanterns around the room.)

HELGA: *(cautiously)* It is not always a good thing, Kirsten, to expect the best . . .

KIRSTEN: You watch and see, Helga. Roosevelt will do something. Why, he's only been president less than a year now, and he's started lots of new government programs!

HELGA: *(more doubtful about the future)* Well, Kirsten, at least we are still holding on. *(She reaches into her* *pocket for a letter.)* Did I tell you, though, what's happened to my brother Ingmar and his family in Baltimore?

KIRSTEN: *(cautiously)* I hope they are well.

HELGA: I just got the news. Ingmar has lost his job at the factory. The Depression's really sunk its teeth into the cities back east, I guess.

KIRSTEN: What will they do?

HELGA: Ingmar and Loni have to leave their little apartment on Charles Street. They've lived there ever since they got married. The landlord says they must be out by the end of the month, or he'll put all their things on the sidewalk!

KIRSTEN: Oh, Lord, Helga, I am so sorry! Do you think your brother and his family could come out here to Kansas? *(She reaches into the cabinet to find dishes to set the table.)* Hmmm. *(half-muttering to herself)* There's so much dust in here. Everything is gritty— the dishes, the table . . . *(turning her attention back to Helga)* Would you have room for Ingmar and his family at the farm?

HELGA: Oh, he would never come out west, Kirsten, especially now that the dust storms have set in. Why, we may end up worse off than them!

(Outside, the wind is rising.)

KIRSTEN: Just listen to it now! I think we may have another big blow tonight, Helga.

(The front door bursts open with a gust of wind, and Nils and Tom hurry in. Nils is burly, about six feet tall, with sandy hair going gray and a wide, open, honest face.

Tom is lanky, athletic, almost as tall as his father, with light brown hair.)

NILS: Kirsten, have you heard—?

KIRSTEN: Oh, Nils, I began to think—

TOM: Mom, turn on the radio quick!

HELGA: What's wrong, Nils? What's going on?

NILS: *(recovering himself a little)* They're talking about a new black blizzard coming this way! It's already buried 'em in the next county.

TOM: *(turning the radio dial)* Shhhh, Dad!

RADIO ANNOUNCER: *(fading up)*—perhaps the most severe dust storm in recent memory! Here in Oklahoma City, street lights have been on since one o'clock in the afternoon. There have been reports from our bureau in Wichita of people in the center of town vomiting from the dust. This evening's forecast is calling for winds over sixty miles an hour on the plains for at least the next twenty-four hours. You are urged to stay indoors and not to undertake any unnecessary travel. In three counties of southwestern Kansas, a state of emergency has been declared—

NILS: Turn that thing off, Tom! No one has to tell us we have an emergency on our hands.

HELGA: *(anxiously)* Oh Kirsten, if we're going to have a storm tonight, I have to get home right away!

NILS: We'll take you back to your house, Helga. Tom and I will just have time on the way back here to stake the new line of saplings.

HELGA: Let me get my kerchief. I'll be ready in a minute.

NILS: *(turning towards Kirsten)* Kirsten, while we're gone you start plugging the keyholes with oilcloth. Stuff newspapers as tight as you can around the windowsills, too. We'll have supper when we get back.

KIRSTEN: But Nils, where's Karen? It's nearly five-thirty, and she's never this late.

TOM: Mom, don't you remember? On Wednesdays she's got piano after school. She'll be OK. If we see her on the road, we'll pick her up. But we've got to get going now if we're to get Mrs. Ulfung home and stake the trees before this wind goes out of control—

NILS: Have you got everything you came with, Helga?

HELGA: *(hurrying to get her sweater, her knitting, and some magazines together)* Yes, Nils, I'm ready. It's good of you to give me a ride in this weather.

NILS: Only three miles from our house to yours, Helga, but it'd feel like thirty trying to make it on foot in this wind. Well, then, let's not lose any time. Kirsten, we'll hope to be back in under an hour . . .

KIRSTEN: Goodbye, Helga. Give Axel a big hug from all of us. And Nils, watch out for Karen on your way . . .

NILS: Of course we will, honey! Now, don't worry. We've been through these storms before . . .

(Door closes on the three of them. Sound of car starting. Kirsten returns to the table in the center of the room and fiddles restlessly with the empty dishes. She turns the radio on and tries to tune the dial to the news again, but all she can get is static. After several minutes, the front

door bursts open again and Karen, thin and blond, is blown in with the dust.)

KAREN: Oh, Mom, it's like a whirlwind out there!

KIRSTEN: Oh, darling, I'm so glad you're home. We've been so worried!

KAREN: You should see the clouds out there. They're like something out of a nightmare.

KIRSTEN: Well, let's hope those clouds don't turn into a real-life nightmare. Now help me finish setting the table. Then you can tell me all about how Miss Johnston liked your new piano piece.

(As mother and daughter busy themselves, we hear the wind still rising to almost a roar. Blackout.)

ACT TWO

The Bergman farmhouse, six months later, May 1934. The interior shows many signs of the family's struggle against the dust storms and of the severe impact of the Depression. There is far less furniture in the room, and some chairs are covered with makeshift dropcloths for protection against the dust. It is late evening. Nils sits reading the paper at the supper table by the light of a kerosene lantern, while Kirsten occupies a nearby rocker, trying to busy herself with a pile of mending. Both have trouble concentrating.

KIRSTEN: See anything in the paper, honey?

NILS: *(sighing deeply)* The news never changes. They're talking about another bad storm for Saturday.

KIRSTEN: How can it go on like this? You'd think we'd had a full plate of sadness this winter. Nils, didn't you tell me that a lot of this trouble goes back to the changeover from cattle raising to growing wheat after the world war?

NILS: That's what this college man said at the growers' meeting last year. The country's so flat now that there is nothing to hold the soil down when you get a big storm. That's why we put in those rows of saplings, remember?

KIRSTEN: Seems like those poor little trees haven't helped us much, though.

NILS: The dust was so high in the shed today that I had to shovel out the tractor.

HELGA: You just did that last week.

NILS: Yeah. *(dejected)* There sure was a lot of dust.

(He turns the pages of the newspaper idly, without really reading. There is a long, somewhat awkward, pause.)

KIRSTEN: Nils, honey, I hate to ask, but Tom's going to need a new pair of shoes.

NILS: Didn't we just get the children some clothes?

KIRSTEN: Last week, your cousin Frieda was able to give me some hand-me-downs that her boys had worn. Before Helga and Axel went out west, Helga left me some clothes for Karen. But we're going to have to do something about the holes in Tom's shoes.

NILS: Well, how much will a new pair cost, then?

KIRSTEN: I can't get them for less than four dollars, honey. Not even secondhand.

NILS: *(bursting out in anger and disbelief)* Four dollars! Four dollars for shoes? Why, Kirsten, four dollars is all we're making now on an acre of wheat! *(Ashamed of his angry reaction, he buries his head in his hands.)*

(Kirsten slowly gets up from her chair, moves to the table, and puts her arm around her husband's shoulders.)

KIRSTEN: Nils, I've been thinking. We have to face it. The time has come. When Axel and Helga left for California, you said that you would never follow. But we can't go on. It's not just the shoes. It's everything. Let's go now while we still can.

NILS: *(slowly raising his head and turning around to face her)* And just throw it all away, Kirsten? The land, the hopes, the dreams?

KIRSTEN: *(gently)* The land has turned to dust, Nils. It's time for different dreams.

NILS: *(beginning to recognize that his wife is right)* Where will we go?

KIRSTEN: *(drawing a deep breath)* We'll go west. We'll go to California, Nils. We'll sell everything except the car, and we'll pay our bills before we leave.

NILS: A new start.

KIRSTEN: Yes, Nils, a new start! Like Papa Gunnar. You remember your father's old stories about pulling up stakes in Sweden?

NILS: Lord, yes! And it sure wasn't easy for them.

KIRSTEN: But Papa Gunnar was right. He said that after he'd made the boat trip west to America, he realized something. He said he found out that when one door closes, another one usually opens—sometimes a better one. Now it's time for us to make a journey west. As long as we have each other, darling, we'll find an open door.

NILS: *(rises and puts his arms around her)* We'll tell the children in the morning.

(They embrace. Blackout.)

ACT THREE

Somewhere on Route 66, just outside Barstow, California. Late June 1934. It is after sunset, about 9:00 P.M., but still blisteringly hot. Throughout the scene, the sounds of cars and trucks on the highway can be heard. The Bergmans have parked their rattletrap 1925 Dodge about 100 feet off the highway by the bank of a small stream. They are unpacking their possessions for the night.

TOM: Where do you want this box, Mom?

KIRSTEN: Well, tell me what's in it, son, and I'll tell you where it goes.

TOM: Looks like kitchen stuff, mostly.

KIRSTEN: Put it over close to where Dad and Karen are spreading out the big blanket. We might need some of what's in it when I make supper.

NILS: *(getting the blanket spread evenly where they'll have supper)* OK, that's good, Karen. Now where's the other blanket for under the car?

KAREN: Come on, Dad. You remember, don't you? It's two whole weeks since we started sleeping out on the road! *(He opens the trunk and brings out another blanket.)*

NILS: My memory must be going, sweetheart. Come on, now. Enough teasing! Let's get it ready.

(They shake out the blanket. Then Nils crawls underneath the car and spreads it out smoothly.)

KAREN: How long do you think we'll have to use the car for sleeping, Dad?

NILS: I don't really know, honey. Maybe another week or two. We're inside California now, and we haven't got that much farther to go.

KAREN: Well, I don't care, as long as it's summer. It's kind of like an adventure—like being off camping or hiking, the way I've seen in those pictures in the *Saturday Evening Post*.

TOM: At least you get to sleep inside the car, Sis, not under it!

KAREN: Come on, Tommy, quit complaining. I told you I'd switch with you any time, and now you're—

KIRSTEN: Children, mind your manners, now. No disagreements at the end of the day, when your father is dead tired from driving. Come, now, let's get ready for a nice supper. *(She turns toward Karen.)* I think you're absolutely right, dear. It's like camping out. So what if we don't have the money to pay for a motel. Let's pretend we're on a camping trip!

TOM: You really think we're going to like it here in California, don't you, Mom?

KIRSTEN: I don't just think so, Tommy. I know it! No more cold nights for us! We're going to have a brand new life! Just you wait and see. You and Karen are going to love it here!

TOM: Sure, Mom. But the people we've met so far haven't exactly been that friendly. Did you see how those fellows looked at us when we stopped for gas at the border this afternoon?

NILS: *(overhearing)* Well, son, people in most parts of the country are suspicious of strangers. And there's more than the usual share of stealing going on now, what with everyone so poor—

KAREN: *(agreeing with her brother)* Yeah, Dad, but I heard one of those mean-looking men say to the other fellow that there ought to be a border fence to keep the Okies out. They hate us, don't they?

(Before Nils can answer, we hear a screech of tires as a vehicle comes to a halt. Loud voices off stage.)

NILS: *(He gestures urgently to Kirsten and Karen.)* Quick! Get under the car!

KIRSTEN: But Nils, we haven't even—

NILS: *(whispering urgently)* There's no time, Kirsten! Just take the girl and do as I say!

(Tom quickly crosses over center stage to be near his father. As Kirsten and Karen roll out of sight, four young men enter stage left. They are poorly dressed, unshaven, scraggly. Two bullies are armed with sticks, and two of them brandish baseball bats.)

JEETER: *(with exaggerated, slow mockery)* Well, now, what have . . . we . . . here? It sure looks to me like what we got is some Okies, Harris.

HARRIS: *(wrinkling his nose)* I'd say it not only looks like it, Jeeter. It also SMELLS like it! *(He laughs roughly at what he thinks is a clever joke.)*

THIRD BULLY: How come they didn't turn these cockroaches back at the border?

NILS: Just a moment, there! We're people, not bugs. And we have just as much right to be here as you fellows! We're not bothering anyone.

FOURTH BULLY: *(mimics Nils insultingly)* Oh, "We're not bothering anybody," are we? Well, you've already bothered me, buster. You know how?

NILS: How could we be bothering you, friend? We're minding our own business.

THIRD BULLY: I think my buddy means that you're bothering him just by being here, you no-good Okie!

TOM: Now just wait one minute—

JEETER: *(advances threateningly)* Well, lookee here, it's Joe High School Okie taking up for his daddy. *(to Nils)* What's the matter, Daddy, can't stand on your own two feet?

NILS: How's this a fair fight, four against two?

HARRIS: Who said anything about fairness, you low-down Okie bum?

(Harris slashes at Nils with his stick. Nils meets the blow with his arm and just barely avoids an injury to his head.)

TOM: *(springing into action to defend his father)* Why, you lousy—

JEETER: Batter up, Harris! Let's get 'em!

(Fighting breaks out. Nils and Tom are holding their own against the bullies until Jeeter runs off and reappears, waving a can full of kerosene, which he empties over the

hood of the Dodge. Tom has darted to the trunk to get out the tire iron, but he's too late. Trying to protect the car, Nils is cracked on the arm by a baseball bat. Howling with pain, he lurches away from the car. Harris strikes a match, throws it on the hood of the car, and jumps back. With a loud whooshing noise, the car catches fire. Laughing insanely, the bullies run offstage, jeering at Nils and Tom, who stare at the burning car in open-mouthed horror. Suddenly, Nils remembers the rest of his family.)

NILS: Oh, God! Kirsten! Karen! Can you hear me? For God's sake, quick! Karen, get out from under the car!

TOM: Mom, can you hear? The car's on fire! Get out from under! *(panics)* God, Dad, what if the car—

(Suddenly, Kirsten and Karen run in from stage right. Their clothes are drenched.)

KIRSTEN: Oh, Nils, honey, are you all right?

KAREN: Are they gone, Tom?

(Tom is busy pushing the burning car into the stream to salvage what he can.)

TOM: Move back! The gas tank could blow any minute!

NILS: *(hugging Kirsten with his left arm, while his right hangs limply at his side)* They're gone, I think. Thank God you're safe.

(Offstage we hear the sound of hissing as the fire is extinguished.)

KAREN: As soon as Mom knew there was going to be a fight, she rolled me out from under, and we fell straight into the water.

NILS: That's my girls! I don't think they even knew you were here.

KIRSTEN: *(noticing his arm)* But Nils, you're hurt! Your arm—

NILS: It's not too painful. See, I don't think it's broken. *(He tries to bend his arm, but cannot.)*

(Offstage, the sound of another vehicle coming to a sharp halt. The family freezes in horror.)

KIRSTEN: Oh no, not again!

TOM: *(decisively)* Mom, Dad, if that's them, you and Karen run toward the road and try to flag down a car, while I hold them off with this. *(He brandishes the tire iron.)*

(Before they can make any further plans, a single man enters stage left. He is short, stocky, balding, about fifty, wearing a khaki shirt and trousers.)

SAMMY: You folks have an accident?

NILS: Well, you could say that. We just met some mighty unfriendly people.

SAMMY: *(He looks around, taking in the whole scene and spots the Kansas license plate on the car.)* Seems like you're traveling quite a ways from home.

NILS: *(quietly)* We don't have a home anymore, mister.

SAMMY: *(nods understandingly)* Dust Bowl, huh—?

(Nils and Kirsten nod their heads in silence.)

SAMMY: Well, the world is full of people looking for a new home, and most of 'em wind up in California. *(He chuckles a little.)* You could say I'm one of 'em.

Our family came all the way from Japan. *(He holds out his hand.)* I'm Sammy. Sammy Nakasone.

(Nils nods, and Kirsten holds out her hand.)

KIRSTEN: We're pleased to meet you, Mr. Nakasone. I'm Kirsten Bergman, and this is my husband Nils. And these are our children, Tom and Karen.

SAMMY: *(smiles and bows)* Call me Sammy. Please call me Sammy.

(Nils tries to shake hands but winces with pain and takes a step back.)

SAMMY: By the looks of that arm, Nils, you're hurt pretty bad.

KIRSTEN: We think it may be broken.

SAMMY: *(to Nils)* You need to get to a doctor.

NILS: But the car, and all our things—

SAMMY: *(looking around again)* That car of yours is goin' nowhere. My pickup's at the side of the road. Plenty of room for you and your stuff. Let's round up everything you want to take, and I'll give you a ride to the clinic in Barstow.

NILS: *(overcome with gratitude)* Thank you, Mr. Nakasone. Thank you very much.

(As the family starts to pick up their possessions, the lights fade down slowly.)

ACT FOUR

A migrant labor camp on the outskirts of San Bernardino, California, six weeks later. Late afternoon. There are tents pitched around the stage. The radiator grills and backs of banged-up cars and pickup trucks are visible. Families are huddled together around small campfires. Small children run in and out of the tents laughing and playing. Nils and Kirsten sit talking. Nils's right arm is in a sling.

KIRSTEN: Maybe tomorrow, darling. Maybe tomorrow someone will say yes.

NILS: Well, let's hope so, Kirsten. But every time a grower sees this sling, he says no to me.

KIRSTEN: I believe it, but Nils, you've got to be patient.

NILS: You'll see, I'll be able to use the arm in a couple of days.

KIRSTEN: Yes, you'll get a job soon. We've had better luck than we've had any right to expect, what with Sammy being able to get us in here.

NILS: Oh, there's no denying that. Why, if Sammy didn't work for the state agricultural agency, we might never have gotten out of that squatters' camp.

KIRSTEN: What an awful place. I was beginning to lose hope for us.

NILS: We owe that Sammy Nakasone a lot.

KIRSTEN: And with Tommy and me picking cotton, and Karen earning a little money baby-sitting, we can get by.

NILS: *(stoutly)* Well, a man should support his family.

(He pauses a moment.) Besides, school's gonna start soon, and the kids will have to quit work.

KIRSTEN: *(hesitates for a second)* After what we've gone through here, I'm not sure that Tom and Karen even want to start school. There's a lot of hard feelings about us Dust Bowl families, and you know how mean kids can be.

NILS: *(breaking in on her, shaking his head)* We can't give in to that, Kirsten. You know their future depends on their education.

KIRSTEN: *(agreeing)* You're right, honey. But can you talk to Tom about it? I know Karen will be all right, but I can't seem to get through to our son.

NILS: I'll talk to him tonight when he gets home from work.

SAMMY: *(sticking his head through an opening in one of the tents)* Knock! Knock!

NILS: Come in!

(Sammy enters briskly and comes forward to shake hands with Kirsten.)

NILS: Why, Sammy, we were just talking about you.

SAMMY: I thought I'd stop by on the way home from the office. How are you making out?

KIRSTEN: Oh, Sammy, we can't thank you enough. This place is so comfortable! After so many weeks, to have showers and fresh water—

NILS: And we're starting to make friends. There are even a few families here who knew relatives of ours back in Kansas.

SAMMY: I'm happy for you, Nils. Sometimes it can be hard getting started in a new place.

KIRSTEN: Sammy, you've done so much for us, I hate to ask you for one more favor.

SAMMY: Don't be silly, Kirsten. It is an honor to help strangers—I mean, you are my new friends.

KIRSTEN: *(looking at Nils)* Nils, honey, do you remember the things we decided we'd sell if we had to?

NILS: *(nodding and reaching into his pocket)* Yes, the time has come. *(He turns to Sammy and hands him a ring with a semiprecious stone on it and a silver pocket watch.)* Sammy, we want the kids to start school here. I'm hoping to get a job in the fields any day now, but I think we may need a little extra money to tide us over. Can you take these to a pawnbroker and get whatever they'll bring?

SAMMY: Of course, Nils. I will do my best.

KIRSTEN: I know you will, Sammy.

NILS: Just don't say anything about it to the children.

(Sammy nods his head and exits silently. Just as he has disappeared and the Bergmans are ready to sit down again, Karen bursts in from stage left.)

KAREN: Oh, Mom! I've just come from Mrs. Olafson's. Little Rita's cough has gotten a lot worse, and Mrs. Olafson wants to take her to the clinic, but her husband's out picking. Shouldn't we go with them?

KIRSTEN: I'm coming, Karen, just let me get my purse. *(She grabs a bag from the table.)* We'll be back to make supper, Nils.

(Mother and daughter exit stage left. Nils sinks into a chair and opens a newspaper. After a few moments, we hear Tom's voice outside, calling like a newsboy, "Extra! Extra!" Then he calls, "Anybody home?" In a moment, he bounds into the room.)

TOM: Guess what, Dad? Great news! Mr. Summers gave me a raise!

NILS: That's wonderful, son.

TOM: It's not much, Dad, only 10 cents a day. But it means I'm up to $6.50 a week, starting next Monday.

NILS: I'm proud of you, son. Sit down for a minute and let's talk. I know you're not exactly keen to go back to school, Tom. What you've done the past few weeks—all summer in fact—has made your parents so proud of you. You've held our family together and done it like a man. But school's starting in three weeks, Tom, and I want you to go.

TOM: But how can I keep on earning money, Dad, if I have to go to school?

NILS: Your mother and I are going to be getting some extra money, son. I'm going back to work in a few days.

TOM: That's great, Dad, but I still don't like the thought of school. We just don't seem to fit in with a lot of these other kids.

NILS: *(after a brief pause)* Tom, have you ever wondered how many different ways there are of being brave? Sometimes, courage is in our bodies. You had that kind of courage when you stood up to those bullies on the road. But sometimes we have to be brave with our minds, like when Papa Gunnar set out from

Sweden for America. This is a time when I want you to be brave with your mind, son.

TOM: *(thinks over what his father has said and then smiles.)* OK, Dad, you win. But if I hear the word "Okie," don't be surprised if I'm in a fight by the end of the first week.

(Nils chuckles and extends his left hand.)

NILS: Shake on it?

TOM: It's a deal, Dad.

(There is a long pause, during which father and son seem lost in thought. Then Tom turns to Nils.)

TOM: *(quietly)* I just have one question, Dad. Why do you think they hate us so much?

NILS: *(gently)* Because they're afraid, son.

(Father and son embrace, and the lights fade down. At the blackout, as from a radio, the voice of President Franklin Delano Roosevelt is heard. The words are those of his first inaugural address: "This great nation will endure as it has endured, will revive and will prosper. So, first of all, let me assert my firm belief that the only thing we have to fear . . . is FEAR ITSELF!")

READING FOR UNDERSTANDING

1. Kirsten stuffs newspapers around the windowsills to keep out the **(a)** cold **(b)** dust **(c)** ants.

2. Nils had planted trees on his land in order to **(a)** provide shade **(b)** produce lumber **(c)** hold down the soil.

3. The Bergmans have little furniture because **(a)** they had to sell it **(b)** they gave it to their neighbors **(c)** it had been damaged in a flood.

4. On the journey west, the Bergmans sleep **(a)** near the highway **(b)** in cabins **(c)** at campgrounds.

5. The moment of greatest danger comes when the Bergmans encounter **(a)** Sammy Nakasone **(b)** the sheriff **(c)** a group of hoodlums.

6. Nils has trouble finding work because of his **(a)** age **(b)** injury **(c)** boastful attitude.

7. In the 1930s, crop prices were **(a)** lower than usual **(b)** higher than usual **(c)** about the same as in the past.

8. You can assume from the play that children of migrant farmers often **(a)** worked for no wages **(b)** lived away from their families **(c)** did not attend school.

RESPONDING TO THE PLAY

1. Which character in the play impressed you the most? What qualities did this character show that made him or her stand out? In a paragraph, write about what you like most about this character. Also, describe your reactions to this character.

2. Toward the end of the play, Nils talks to his son about a courage that means "being brave with our minds." What do you think this means? Do you

know anyone who has shown this kind of courage? Describe this person and this special courage.

REVIEWING VOCABULARY

The following sentences are based on the play. Decide which of the words following the sentences best fits each blank. Write your answers on a separate sheet of paper.

1. To reduce some of the damage caused by windstorms, farmers planted _____ on their land.
2. Sammy Nakasone helps the Bergmans move out of their _____ housing in a squatters' camp into a house with indoor plumbing.
3. The Bergmans hoped that their _____ Dodge would last long enough to get them to California.
4. Nils gives Sammy a watch and a ring to take to a _____ for money to help his family manage.
5. Kirsten is a _____ woman who has the strength to survive hard times.

Words: *pawnbroker, abandoned, robust, saplings, expensive, makeshift, rattletrap*

THINKING CRITICALLY

1. Kirsten compares the Bergmans' move to her father-in-law's move from Sweden to the United States. In what way are the two moves similar? In what way might they be different?
2. Why do you think some Californians hated the Okies?
3. Sammy Nakasone is a Japanese American. These people faced prejudice, as many of the Okies did. Do you think this influenced his decision to help the Bergmans? Why or why not?

4. In the end, Nils urges his son to return to school. He does this even though the family needs the money that Tom earns. What does this tell you about Nils and the values he has?

5. What are your feelings at the end of the play? What do you think will happen to the Bergmans? Discuss how events and characters in the play lead you to feel the way you do.

WRITING PROJECTS

1. Write a new scene about Tom's first day at school. Use what you know about Tom and about Californians' attitudes toward "Okies" to create your scene. Develop a sketch of the characters and outline the main events in your scene before you begin writing.

2. Reporters traveled to the camps of migrant farm-workers in California. They documented the suffering of farm families like the Bergmans. Put yourself in the place of one of those reporters. Write a newspaper article describing the life of a migrant farm family.

Help Wanted

Joyce Haines

Would you be surprised to see a woman building an airplane or working in an office? Probably not. Today, the idea of a woman working outside the home is not at all unusual. In the 1940s, it was very unusual. Before World War II, most women—especially married women—did not hold jobs. The war changed all that.

Millions of men had to leave their jobs to fight in the war. Factories and offices across the nation called on women to take the places of these men. Women workers produced much of what the United States and its allies needed to win the war. They made everything from tanks and airplanes to shoes and belts. But they often were paid less than men for the same jobs.

Many women found that they enjoyed working. They were proud to be helping their country and supporting their families. However, many people resented these women. They felt that women should not be in the work-force. As you read this play, notice how the women struggle to break away from their old roles.

VOCABULARY WORDS

turban (TER-buhn) a scarf or bandanna tied around the head
❖ She wore a *turban* to protect her hair from getting caught in machines.

propellant (proh-PEHL-uhnt) the explosive charge that causes a bomb to explode or a weapon to fire
❖ The women worked mixing *propellant* for bombs.

solvents (SAHL-vuhnts) liquids that can break down other liquids
❖ Since the *solvents* were so powerful, we wore gloves when working with them.

gaseous (GAS-ee-uhs, GASH-uhs) in the form of gas
❖ After the explosion at the chemical plant, the building was filled with *gaseous* fumes.

tirades (TY-radz) long, angry speeches
❖ It was hard to predict when he would go on one of his *tirades* and begin yelling at the employees.

diminished (duh-MIHN-ihsht) lessened, reduced
❖ What the flood victims want is *diminished* rainfall.

expendable (ehks-PEHN-duh-buhl) unnecessary; able to be replaced or given up
❖ The workers were laid off because their services were *expendable*.

KEY WORD

Aleutian (uh-LOO-shuhn) **Islands** chain of islands southwest of Alaska
❖ The *Aleutian Islands* stretch over 1,000 miles in the Pacific Ocean near Alaska.

CHARACTERS

Rosemary Wright, *employee at Sunflower Ordnance Works*

Tom Miller, *supervisor at Sunflower Ordnance Works*

Sue Goodwin, *employee at Sunflower Ordnance Works*

Ann, *assembly line worker*

Jane, *assembly line worker*

Several other women employees

George Harshman, *general manager*

SETTING

Act One
A box-making room at Sunflower Ordnance Works, March 1943

Act Two
Scene 1
The "Mix House" st Sunflower Ordnance Works, December 1943

Scene 2
The Sunflower cafeteria, February 1944

Act Three
Scene 1
The factory X-ray room, August 1945

Scene 2
The factory X-ray room, January 1946

ACT ONE

A **large, noisy box-making room** *at the Sunflower Ordnance Works in Eudora, Kansas. A calendar on the wall is turned to March 1943. The calendar shows a picture of a mother and child, and the words*

"Protect your loved ones. Buy war bonds."

Rosemary Wright enters the room and walks slowly toward the group of workers. She is a young Kansas farm woman, about 22 years old. Sue, Anne, and Jane stand at an assembly line. Row after row of short pine boards move along the line. The women nail them together to construct ammunition powder boxes. Each one wears gray overalls. The women wear turbans. Tom Miller, their 25-year-old line supervisor, stands behind them with his hands on his hips. He frowns as Rosemary approaches.

TOM: *(yelling)* What's that? Speak up . . . I can't hear you.

ROSEMARY: *(tentative and confused, but attempting to shout)* I said, my name is Rosemary Wright. They told me to talk to you about a job. *(As she speaks, the background noise gradually fades.)*

TOM: Are you Bill Wright's little sister? Man, oh, man. He's the one we need here. That guy can get a job done.

ROSEMARY: *(proudly)* We just got a letter from Bill before he got shipped out to the Pacific. He's already a corporal. John, my oldest brother—he just got promoted to lieutenant in the Navy. Bobby is only fifteen, or else he'd be—

TOM: *(cuts her off and shrugs his shoulders)* Well, let's go see what you can do for us. You don't look strong enough to push a buggy. You might as well start over there, where we put together the powder boxes. Do you think you can handle that? *(Rosemary nervously nods yes.)* You have to make at least forty boxes an hour. It shouldn't be too hard for Bill's little sister, should it? Just watch Sue and do exactly what she does. Here, put on these overalls and turban. They'll protect you from the chemicals. *(He picks up the clothes from a nearby bench, hands them to Rosemary, then looks at the clock on the wall. It is 9:00 A.M.)* Tomorrow, try to get here on time. You're already an hour late. By the way, don't forget that this is swing-shift work. That means you have to work from midnight until eight A.M. two weeks out of every six. *(Tom looks at her angrily. As he walks away, Rosemary notices that he is limping.)*

ROSEMARY: But, but—

SUE: Don't let him bother you. He's always complaining. We just have to work around him. *(proudly)* Our section has been ahead of schedule since the beginning.

ROSEMARY: But I was trying to tell him that I came to apply for a job as a file clerk. I've never worked in a factory before, only at the library. Then I had to drop out of college to help my family. I don't know why the office sent me over here.

SUE: Why don't you give it a try? Besides, this job pays seventy-four cents an hour. That's five cents more than you can make in the office. *(She sighs.)* Of course, it's a dime less than any of the men make for the same job.

ROSEMARY: Well, it is for the war. *(She picks up a hammer and starts pounding nails into the wood, along with the other women.)* What did he mean about my not being strong enough to push a buggy?

SUE: *(She points to a huge steel cart on the other side of the room.)* That's the buggy. The workers down the

137

line load the boxes into it. Then they have to push it over to Building C, where they fill them with the propellant powder. The rules are that women workers can't lift anything over thirty-five pounds, and we can't push the buggy alone. We have to have two women for each buggy. Otherwise, we do the same work as the men.

ANN: *(She gestures with her head, not looking away from a work table where she is packaging small boxes into large boxes.)* See Mrs. Melton over there, loading those boxes into the buggy?

ROSEMARY: You mean that woman with the gray hair?

ANN: Yes, she has five children, ages five to twenty-three, and six grandchildren. This is the first job she's ever had besides housekeeping, and she works better than any of us. Maybe you read about her in the local newspaper last week. It was a nice article about the women workers. Sixty percent of us here are women.

ROSEMARY: No, I didn't see it. I live fifty miles away, outside Kansas City.

JANE: So you're one of the group that comes in by train. What time do you have to leave home in the morning?

ROSEMARY: I get up at five o'clock to walk to the train station. The train leaves at six-fifteen, but it makes a lot of stops along the way. I'll be lucky to get home by seven-thirty tonight. I might as well stay in my pajamas.

JANE: *(She quickly "models" her uniform.)* Nobody here would see any difference.

(They all laugh.)

ROSEMARY: How long have you girls been working here? Where do you live?

SUE: I've been here two months. I take the bus in from a farm west of town. It takes me an hour and a half. Also, the bus makes a lot of stops. *(yawning)* Sure makes for a long workday, doesn't it?

TOM: *(walking up to Sue, with his hands on his hips again)* I said you should show her the ropes. I didn't give you gals the OK to have a ladies' social. Get to work. We have a production schedule to keep. We're not here for laughs, girls. *(He walks away, scowling, as the women work faster.)*

SUE: *(whispering)* He's the only one of his high school class that didn't make it into the army. He's awfully sensitive about it. So he tries to take it out on us. Try not to talk about where your brothers are fighting when Tom's around. He doesn't want to hear about the war.

JANE: *(She sighs.)* I hope this war ends soon. It's so lonely now, especially without Mark.

ROSEMARY: Who's Mark? No, I guess you don't have to tell me. Are you engaged? *(pause)* Where's he stationed?

JANE: He's also somewhere in the Pacific right now. We're going to get married as soon as he returns. What about you? Where's your guy?

ROSEMARY: There's no one special, yet. I live in such a small town, and now everyone's gone. My grandmother says not to worry. She says I take after her grandmother—the first and last woman in our family ever to work outside the home. They say we even look alike. I sure wish I'd known her.

SUE: What did this great-grandmother do?

ROSEMARY: She worked in a cotton mill in Lowell, Massachusetts. After work hours, she started a mill school to help the younger girls get a high school education. The town actually named a school in her honor.

SUE: She sounds like my kind of heroine. Self-made. Not afraid to break away. Like Bessie Coleman, the black woman aviator. She had to go all the way to France for her flight training. But she got her pilot's license in 1921. Bessie was getting ready to start a flying school for other black people when her plane crashed in 1926. *(Sue is quiet for a moment, then looks across the room and out the window.)* And, of course, there was Amelia.

ROSEMARY: Amelia?

ANN: *(sarcastically)* Oh boy. Bring out the soapbox. Step right up, Sue.

SUE: *(ignoring Ann)* Amelia Earhart, naturally, our own Kansas heroine. It's been eleven years since she became the first woman to fly solo across the Atlantic. *(excited)* I've visited her home in Atchison.

JANE: *(smiling)* You should see Sue's collection of photos and clippings. She's got the history of every female pilot that ever lived.

SUE: *(excitedly)* Now that Amelia's gone, Jackie Cochran and dozens like her are flying. I want to be out there flying with them. I swear I'll do it. *(She calms down a bit.)* I have to stay close to home for

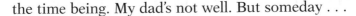

the time being. My dad's not well. But someday . . .

ROSEMARY: Well, it sounds better than being a farm wife in Kansas. But I think I'd like to be a chemistry teacher. I love science—solving problems. Finding out what makes things happen. That's what I want to do when this war's over. When do you—*(She is interrupted by the sound of an alarm.)*

SUE: *(flatly)* It's OK. That's just the safety alarm. It's like a fire drill. *(pause)* Of course, this place could blow sky high.

(They begin to walk out.)

ACT TWO, SCENE 1

Rosemary and Sue are working together in the Sunflower "Mix House." Sue is adjusting a machine that mixes solvents to create the explosives needed for the war. A gaseous vapor drifts up from huge copper vats. Rosemary is measuring exact proportions and recording the measurements in a log book. The calendar behind them is turned to December 1943.

SUE: I'm glad you talked me into taking that business course and taking this job. *(Rosemary makes a dismissive gesture.)* Thanks, really. I'm glad to get away from pounding nails into boxes. At least it's quiet here. I couldn't stand another minute of that factory noise. But I don't know how safe this work is.

ROSEMARY: Don't worry. I made it my business to study the mixtures very carefully in Dr. Brewster's chemistry course. I've learned more about chemistry in that eight-week course and this last month on the job than I ever could in a regular college classroom.

SUE: Then why don't you tell us what this stuff is. It sure stinks.

ROSEMARY: It's supposed to. *(then, in a German accent)* But if you follow my orders, you vill not be hurt.

SUE: What's in it, anyway?

ROSEMARY: It's a mixture of sulfuric acid and nitric acid, with a very small amount of nitroglycerine. This makes the smokeless propellant powder that's needed for the hundred-fifty-five millimeter field guns and howitzers. *(The others move uneasily.)* Don't look so worried. It won't explode until you put it in the shell casing with the cotton linter.

SUE: Okay, professor, what's a cotton linter?

ROSEMARY: That's the short fibers that cling to cotton seeds. Come on, you're going to be a pilot some day. You can't let these things scare you off.

SUE: Well, you're the chemist. *(after a pause)* Have you heard any news from your brothers lately?

ROSEMARY: *(looking troubled)* We've only gotten one letter from each of them since August. That's when we recaptured the Aleutian Islands from the Japanese. We don't even know where they are right now. I just have to keep up my faith that they're safe.

SUE: Look, I know they'll make it home safely. From what you've told me, they're two strong, sharp men. They'll be okay. *(shyly)* Can I tell you a secret?

ROSEMARY: Of course. What is it?

SUE: Do you remember the pen pal I told you about? Well, he's a mechanic in the Army Air Corps. I got his name when I joined the Victory Book campaign and started sending books to the soldiers stationed overseas.

ROSEMARY: Yes, I remember.

SUE: Well, his name is John Baker. He's thirty-two, and he comes from a small town in Maine. We've been writing to each other for almost a year now. Here's his picture. *(pause)* Handsome, isn't he? He's the only man I've ever known who didn't make fun of my dream to fly. As soon as the war's over, John wants to come here to visit me. Isn't it exciting?

ROSEMARY: Oh, Sue. That's wonderful. Yes, he looks very impressive. I guess you two may be flying together someday. *(She yawns.)* Sorry, I'm dead tired. Getting up at five in the morning is killing me. By the time I finish the chores at home, it's almost midnight before I get to bed. Thank goodness my little brother is able to help with the farm work. Since my grandmother died last month, my mom has more time to get things done. Taking care of Grandma was a full-time job for her for so long. *(She yawns again.)* I'm so tired, Sue.

SUE: Oh, I meant to tell you. I just heard that they have one dorm left here at Sunflower. It would cost us ten dollars and eighty-five cents each for a double room, with washtubs and a telephone down the hall. We could share a room. How about it?

ROSEMARY: You and me? In a dorm room? Do you talk at night like you do during the day?

SUE: We'd save bus and train money and have a lot more time at the end of the day. It would sure make things easier when we have to work the midnight-to-eight shift. *(She hesitates, sensing Rosemary's lack of* *enthusiasm among the others.)* We could still go home on weekends.

ROSEMARY: I don't know what's worse: the long commute or living in a tent on the Sunflower grounds. There's ten thousand people working here now. Can you imagine? And some people have brought their families. Those women have four or five children living with them in one big tent.

SUE: What do you think about sharing a dorm room? That room won't be available for long.

ROSEMARY: Let's do it. Call the dorm manager on your lunch break. I think my parents will understand. *(She thinks for a moment.)* You know, this will also give me the chance I've wanted to do some good around here. I could teach some basic science to those kids in the tents, after hours.

SUE: That's a great idea. The children have the school across the road, but they need all the individual help they can get.

ROSEMARY: I also have a lot of interesting books from home. Mom used to read to us every night. We could start a reading group for adult women, like they used to do in the old days. We could concentrate on subjects that might help them to get ahead. And if we can get the space from Mr. Harshman, I'll bet I could even get a couple of my old college teachers to drive in one night a week.

SUE: *(smiling and looking up at her)* I can almost hear your great-grandmother cheering you on.

ROSEMARY: Cheering us *both* on, you mean. I can't do it alone, you know. It will mean a lot of hard work for both of us. And who knows if any of the women would have any strength left to read and think after standing on their feet all day? But it's worth a try.

SUE: Who's going to ask Mr. Harshman for the space?

ROSEMARY: I'm not afraid to ask Mr. Harshman. He can't say no to *this* idea.

ACT TWO, SCENE 2

The Sunflower Ordnance Works cafeteria on a February night, 1944. Ann, Jane, and several other women of all ages are seated around two long tables, with notebooks in front of them. They look very tired, but their eyes are bright and eager as they see Rosemary and Sue walking toward them with George Harshman. Somewhat overweight, Harshman walks slowly and seems to have trouble breathing.

(None of the women at the table move.)

GEORGE: *(puffing out his chest and coughing, then standing in front of Rosemary and Sue)* No, don't get up, ladies. I just came to tell you that I've decided to let you continue using the cafeteria, after all. That was some petition you sent me. Three thousand names in favor of your tutoring and book groups. Very impressive. Very impressive, indeed. And that latest newspaper article certainly made us sound good here at Sunflower. Yes, sir. The management has always supported its lady workers. We've worked hard to give the fairer sex every opportunity. You can count on me, ladies. I know you join me in thanking Miss Wright and Miss Goodwin here for their impressive efforts.

SUE: *(whispering to Rosemary)* What a fake. If we didn't force him—

ROSEMARY: *(motioning to Sue to keep quiet)* Thank you, Mr. Harshman. We always appreciate your support.

ANN: This means a lot to us.

GEORGE: I'm sure it does. If there's anything I can do to help you ladies, all you have to do is ask.

SUE: *(whispering to Rosemary)* How about paying us the same as the men doing the same jobs?

GEORGE: Before I let you get on with your studies, I have an announcement. The Army is sending us a special visitor. You may have heard of Jacqueline Cochran, the director of the Women's Airforce Service Pilots. She's on a special recruiting mission. Now, I'd sure hate to lose even one of you, and, frankly, I believe that this factory is exactly where you belong until the war's over. But Miss Cochran is a very determined young lady, and the Army has given her permission to interview any of you girls who might be interested in working with her. She'll be here next week. Stop by the office in Building G if you want to sign up for an interview. Well, that's all. Back to work, ladies. *(He turns abruptly and leaves as the women roll their eyes and suppress smiles.)*

ROSEMARY: Sue, here's your big chance. You might be flying sooner than you expected.

SUE: I can't believe it.

ACT THREE, SCENE 1

Ann, Tom, and Rosemary are working in the factory X-ray room. It is August 1945. Ann is preparing X-ray machinery, while Rosemary examines the developed X-rays of boxed ammunition powder. Tom sits at a desk off to the side, behind a glass partition, shuffling papers.

ANN: *(whispering to Rosemary)* Just look at him. Our foreman. Ha! If he didn't have you around here to explain the chemistry to him and make him look good, he wouldn't have a job at all.

ROSEMARY: *(concentrating on an X-ray analysis)* Quiet. He'll hear you. Let's not get him started on another one of his tirades.

TOM: What's going on over there, Rosie? Did you find another problem?

ROSEMARY: It looks like this one mixture is off. I can see traces of a bit too much nitric acid. Want to have a look?

TOM: Huh? Oh, sure. Let me see. Bring it on over here.

ROSEMARY: *(She walks over to Tom's desk.)* Here, look at these smudges. They shouldn't be there. I'm sure the box is spoiled.

TOM: The plant's behind production schedule. *(shrugging)* It doesn't look like too much damage. I'm going to OK this one.

ROSEMARY: *(standing straight and glaring down at Tom)* No! Absolutely not. What we're doing here means life or death to our soldiers. No compromise on this one.

TOM: *(rattled by her fervor)* All right, Rosie, all right. You win this time. Don't get so worked up. But I'm

147

warning you, the plant has to catch up to the production schedule. I can't afford to let you slow us
down with these darn tests and re-tests.

ROSEMARY: *(quietly and evenly)* We have to do everything we can to protect our soldiers, Mr. Miller, even
if it means falling a little behind schedule.

TOM: Sure, Rosie. Now, go back to work and leave me
alone. Can't you see that I have a lot to do here? *(He
picks up his papers again, then looks out the window
as Rosemary walks away.)*

ANN: *(whispering)* I guess he showed you who's boss,
huh?

ROSEMARY: Oh, I guess he can't help himself. But at
least he's never forced me to OK any shipment that
isn't perfect. He knows what's at stake. Let him take
the credit, if that's what he needs. Just so long as he
lets me do my job.

ANN: I've heard that Tom might get a promotion. Why
don't you apply for his job, Rosemary? You're the
one with the chemistry background, after all.

ROSEMARY: You know, I've been thinking about it. After
all, Mr. Harshman promised that most of us would
be able to keep our jobs even after the war is over.
The government will still need some ammunition on
hand. The only problem is that I'd have a hard time
getting a good recommendation from Tom. You
know how he feels about women workers. In some
ways, he's worse than Mr. Harshman.

ANN: Ability is what matters. You know that better than
anybody here. Look what you and Sue did for all of
us. The after-hours tutoring, the discussion groups,

more women line supervisors, even a pay raise. We're almost getting what the men earn.

ROSEMARY: Thanks. But I'm not sure if Sunflower is ready for a "forewoman" to replace a foreman. By the way, I got a letter from Sue yesterday. She just got her pilot's license. I'll show you her picture later. She looks so proud in her uniform. Can you believe it?

ACT THREE, SCENE 2

The factory X-ray room. It is January 1946. The war is now over. There is a diminished need for factory work- ers at Sunflower. Many veterans who had worked at the factory before the war have reclaimed their former jobs. Ann and Rosemary are still employed at Sunflower, but a third of the staff has been let go. Ann is busy at the X-ray machine. Rosemary examines the developed X-rays. Tom's desk is empty.

ANN: *(She looks up from her work.)* It sure is quiet around here. So many people are gone. I wonder how many more changes Mr. Harshman will make this year.

ROSEMARY: Yeh. A lot of people are wondering the same thing.

ANN: How do you think Tom will do over in the powder press room? He didn't look too happy when he packed up his stuff this morning.

ROSEMARY: He hardly said goodbye. Well, he always was quiet, but I thought he would say something to me about my promotion. After all, Mr. Harshman promised me—*(She stops talking as Mr. Harshman enters the room.)*

ANN: Good afternoon, Mr. Harshman.

GEORGE: Good afternoon, Miss . . . eh . . .

ANN: Stark, Mr. Harshman. My name is Ann Stark. I've worked here five years.

GEORGE: *(turning his back on her)* Oh, right. Say, Rosemary, I thought you'd want to know that I've hired a veteran to replace Tom. He starts next week. In the meantime, I'm sure you can carry on here. Just call Tom if you have any questions. He knows how to handle everything. It sure will be good to have our vets take over so you ladies can go back home where you belong. I guess you're both pretty anxious to get married and start a family. Well, it won't be long, ladies. Life can get back to normal now. *(He turns abruptly and leaves the room.)*

(The two women look at one another. Rosemary shakes her head, obviously disappointed. Then her facial expression resolves to determination.)

ANN: How can they just let us go? We've been here for years!

ROSEMARY: They think we're expendable. Well, it's their loss. We just have to get on with our lives.

ANN: You mean get married and start a family?

ROSEMARY: Yes, if that's what you want. Or be a pilot, a chemist, whatever. But it's our lives we're talking about. Come on, let's get going.

READING FOR UNDERSTANDING

Overview

1. The play takes place at a factory in Kansas during **(a)** World War I **(b)** World War II **(c)** the Vietnam War.

2. The women at the factory are paid **(a)** once a month **(b)** the same as the men **(c)** less than the men.

3. Tom's personality could best be described as **(a)** mellow and pleasant **(b)** silent and reliable **(c)** angry and unfriendly.

Act One

4. Rosemary says that she admires her great-grandmother because she was the last woman in her family to **(a)** work outside the home **(b)** fly an airplane **(c)** do housework.

5. Sue's ambition is to be **(a)** a permanent factory worker **(b)** a sharpshooter **(c)** an aviator.

Act Two

6. Rosemary and Sue look forward to **(a)** careers outside the home **(b)** taking flying lessons **(c)** living together after the war.

7. Mr. Harshman allows Sue and Rosemary to **(a)** work as file clerks **(b)** set up a study group for the women **(c)** use the cafeteria as an exercise room.

Act Three

8. When Tom is about to be promoted, Ann encourages Rosemary to **(a)** apply for Tom's job **(b)** join Sue as a pilot **(c)** complain to Mr. Harshman that Tom is not qualified.

9. From his comments, we can assume that Mr.

Harshman feels that women **(a)** should take every chance for job promotion **(b)** are better workers than men **(c)** should stay at home.

10. After the war, the person who takes Tom's job turns out to be **(a)** Rosemary **(b)** Ann **(c)** a veteran hired by Mr. Harshman.

11. At the end of the play, Rosemary is clearly **(a)** sick of war **(b)** ready for housework **(c)** eager for a career.

RESPONDING TO THE PLAY

1. In Act I Rosemary and Sue describe their heroines. Do you feel that it's important to have a hero or heroine as a role model? Who is your hero or heroine? Write a paragraph telling why he or she is important.

2. Rosemary does not get a promotion at the end of the play. However, she feels that women can be anything they want in life, if they set their minds to it. Do you think this is true? Write a short editorial based on your point of view.

REVIEWING VOCABULARY

The following sentences are based on the play. Decide which of the words following the sentences best fits each blank. Write your answers on a separate sheet of paper.

1. After the war, there was a _____ need for workers at the plant.

2. Tom, who was unhappy with his job, often went on _____ in which he took out his anger on the women workers.

3. Rosemary put on a pair of overalls and a _____ to protect herself from the chemicals.

4. In the Mix House at the factory, a _____ vapor slowly drifted up from huge copper vats.

5. When Rosemary failed to receive her promotion, it was clear that Mr. Harshman thought she was _____.

6. Sue adjusted a machine that mixed _____ to create the explosives needed in the war.

Words: *gaseous, tirades, expendable, diminished, turban, solvents*

THINKING CRITICALLY

1. Why do you think Tom is so unfriendly and sulky?

2. Give some reasons why you think the factory's management paid the women less than the men? Were any of the reasons justified?

3. How does Rosemary show courage during the play? How does she show honesty?

4. What does the play suggest about the importance of education and knowledge?

5. Fifty years after these events, some women workers still have a hard time getting equal pay and fair treatment. In view of this, do you feel that Rosemary was right to behave as she did at the end of the play? Tell why or why not.

WRITING PROJECTS

1. How do you think life turns out for the women in this play? Make a short outline for a sequel to the play that answers this question.

2. How do you think Rosemary would react to today's women's movement? Write a short speech that Rosemary might give to a women's club. Have her recall her problems at Sunflower.

The Amache Trap

Sandra Widener

Think about where you live. Think about your neighborhood and friends. Imagine that you and your family are forced to leave your home. It's hard to believe that something like this could happen in the United States. But it did happen to thousands of Japanese American families during World War II.

After Japan attacked Pearl Harbor in 1941, many Americans feared that Japanese Americans might be spies. So the U.S. government rounded up all the Japanese Americans living on the West Coast and sent them to relocation camps. Living conditions were poor. These Japanese American families suffered greatly.

When the war ended, the Japanese Americans were released. Some found that their homes were gone and their businesses had been taken over by other people. Many moved away from the West Coast.

In 1988, the U.S. government apologized to the Japanese Americans. Each former internee or his or her family got twenty thousand dollars. Do you think money could make up for what happened? Find out how the Goto family felt about being "relocated."

VOCABULARY WORDS

hooligans (HOO-lih-gunhz) hoodlums; people who do bad things
❖ The store owners asked the police to find the *hooligans* who had smashed their windows.

curfew (KER-fyoo) a rule that people must be off the streets at certain times
❖ Once the *curfew* was in effect, the streets were almost empty.

evacuate (ih-VAK-yoo-ate) to remove, especially from a dangerous area
❖ The government decided to *evacuate* all citizens from the war zone.

dramatic (druh-MAT-ihk) in an exaggerated way
❖ I expected a *dramatic* reaction from my friend, but she took the news calmly.

modest (MAH-dihst) not showy or fancy
❖ The writer was rich, yet he chose to live in a *modest* neighborhood.

KEY WORDS

relocation camps (REE-loh-KAY-shun KAMPS) camps set up by the U.S. government's War Relocation Agency (WRA) to hold Japanese Americans during World War II
❖ Often, families of four or five had to live in one room in the *relocation camps*.

internees (ihn-tern-EEZ) persons confined to a specific area in wartime
❖ The Japanese American *internees* were angry that they had been forced to leave their homes.

156

CHARACTERS

Susumu Goto, *father, a Japanese American in his early forties*
Iku Goto, *mother, a Japanese American of the same age*
Keiko Goto, *daughter, age fourteen*
Isamu Goto, *son, age sixteen*
Patrolman 1
Patrolman 2
Official
Hanayo Makabe

SETTING

Act One
The Goto family living room in a Los Angeles, California, suburb

Act Two
Scene 1
The Goto family living room, three days later

Scene 2
The Goto family garage and driveway, several hours later

Act Three
The barracks of the Amache Relocation Camp in Colorado

ACT ONE

Inside the living room of the Goto family's home in a modest Los Angeles suburb. *The furnishings are a mix of Forties deco and Japanese-style furnishings. Its older members, Susumu and Iku, are first-generation Japanese Americans. Their children, Keiko and*

157

Isamu, are teenagers. Susumu wears western clothes. Iku is wearing a housecoat that looks like a kimono. The two teenagers are dressed like teenagers of the period. It is March 24, 1942.

KEIKO: *(opens the door and yells to someone outside.)* Jimmy, you know me! I'm as American as you! I've never even been to Japan, and I wouldn't go if I could. Fine! Fine, if that's the way you feel! Just leave me alone! *(Keiko slams the door.)*

IKU: *(hurrying to her daughter)* Keiko! What is this? Keep your voice down!

KEIKO: I'm sorry, Mom. It's just some kids from school. They've been following me home from school every day, yelling things.

IKU: *(looking worried)* Things? What things?

KEIKO: It's nothing, Mother. I'm sorry I said anything. Just forget about it.

IKU: Keiko, you were screaming. You were upset. Now, you tell me. What were they yelling?

KEIKO: *(reluctantly)* Oh, you know. About being Japanese and everything. Just kids being stupid.

IKU: This has been going on every day?

KEIKO: Look, Mother, it really doesn't matter. It's just everyone is so upset about the war. And then with the Japanese winning all the battles lately, people are—well, you know. They're upset. They're scared.

IKU: It's getting worse. I can't believe what I hear on the radio. People who used to come to the store don't come anymore. I cannot believe they would think of making us live like prisoners. We've been here for so

many years! We pay taxes! We are as American as anyone. We have every right to be here! *(She begins to cry.)* When I see these people attacking you, I don't know what to do. I just don't know.

KEIKO: *(comforting her mother)* This can't last, Mother.

IKU: I know. And I will not give up my home and everything we worked so hard for just to let some hooligans run us out.

(Susumu Goto opens the door and walks into the room, looking troubled.)

KEIKO: Hi, Dad. How are things at the store? You look upset or something.

SUSUMU: Upset? Of course I'm upset. No one is coming to the store now except other Japanese. Every day we lose money. I had to let Rafe go today, and then he accused me of being a dirty Jap. Rafe! Of all people! He should know us by now. *(He sits in a chair, exhausted, and shakes his head.)* I can't take much more. I don't even care what happens at the store anymore. Did you see the latest? *(He pulls a crumpled paper from his pocket and holds it up.)* Do you know what this says? We have a curfew, like dogs or bad children. We can be outside our homes from eight in the morning to six at night. They say they are going to evacuate us somewhere. Soon. This isn't just another threat, either. They sound serious.

IKU: This can't be! They can't do this to citizens!

SUSUMU: *(bitterly)* Citizens? That's a good one. Citizens. We are dogs to them.

KEIKO: Father, not everyone is like that. Remember: the Hendersons still shop at the store. So do the

Michaels. These people are our friends. They—

SUSUMU: *(waving his hands)* I don't want to hear it. We're getting out.

IKU: We can't leave everything we worked years to build! That business is ours! We built it with our hands, with our work. If we go, we are letting others have it all. How can we do that? We should not slink away like rats, like we've done something wrong. Our life is here.

(Isamu walks into the house, holding a piece of paper in his hand identical to the one that Susumu held up.)

ISAMU: *(holding up the paper)* Can you believe this? I'd like to ram this stupid paper down their throats.

IKU: Isamu! I will not have that in this house.

ISAMU: Sorry, Mother. It's just that I was so upset—

IKU: I know, Isamu. I'm angry, too. We were just talking about what to do.

KEIKO: This is just temporary insanity. These people are our friends! We should stay and show them they are wrong about us.

SUSUMU: It's no longer a question of proving anything by staying. If we don't do something, we'll be herded like cattle into a prison camp somewhere. I won't allow that to happen to us.

IKU: Do something? What can we do?

SUSUMU: If they will treat us like criminals, we will act like criminals. *(turning to the children)* Do you remember your cousins in Colorado? Aunt Hanayo has written us a letter. She says their governor,

Governor Carr, will not allow the Japanese in Colorado to be put in camps. She asks us to join them there.

IKU: You want to give up. We cannot do that. Keiko is right. There are some good people here. They will not let this happen to us.

SUSUMU: Good people. Ha! Even if there are, they will be able to do nothing.

ISAMU: I'm with father. These people here don't want us. If we don't leave, we'll be living in camps.

KEIKO: Don't be so dramatic. They'll probably just put us in apartments somewhere. They may not even do that.

IKU: If we try to run away, the government could send us to a real prison. What if they send us to a real prison?

SUSUMU: This is a risk we should take. I don't want to be treated as a criminal. I will not—*(There is the sound of glass shattering, as a rock with a paper tied to it is thrown through the living room window. The family is frozen for a moment. Then Iku gasps, and Susumu stoops to pick up the rock. He unwraps the message and reads it to himself. Then he speaks to Keiko.)* Here are your fine Americans. Would you like to hear what your fine Americans have to say to us? *(reading from the paper that covered the rock)* "Dirty Japs put ground glass in the vegetables they sell. Go back to Japan."

(The family is silent for a moment.)

ISAMU: Father, you are right. Even if we take a risk by leaving, we could be killed if we stay here. At best, we will be sent to camps like we did something wrong. We should go. Now.

SUSUMU: *(looking around at his family)* I want to go to your cousin's in Colorado. This is a serious decision. But, remember this: If we go, we will be acting as people, not as frightened children.

ISAMU: I say go.

KEIKO: I say stay.

IKU: I hate to leave. But if it is true, what Hanayo says about the Japanese in Colorado, maybe we should try to go there. Maybe people would leave us alone there.

SUSUMU: It is settled, then. We will make plans. I think I know someone who will run the store for us while we are gone. Begin packing. We must move quickly. Within a week, we should be in the car and on our way. This place, where people yell at us and throw rocks at our windows, this place is not for us.

ACT TWO, SCENE 1

March 27, late afternoon, inside the Goto family's living room. There are several medium-sized boxes on the stage, and piles of clothing. Members of the family are packing the boxes and carrying armfuls of items.

IKU: Keiko! Keiko! Did you pack the bedding?

KEIKO: Yes, Mother. It's inside that box. *(She points to one of the boxes.)*

IKU: I forgot the special quilt your father likes so much. Would you find it and put it in?

KEIKO: I still haven't packed my things yet, you know.

IKU: Well, get to it. We're leaving tonight. Remember?

KEIKO: Of course I remember! Do you think that I've been sitting around here doing nothing all this time? We shouldn't even be doing this. We're going to get caught, and then we'll all go to jail. My friend Marcy says if we go, we're just proving that all Japanese are bad.

IKU: *(She stops in her work, straightens up, and faces Keiko.)* Do you mean to tell me that you told Marcy we were going to leave? Keiko, how could you? What if she tells someone? Do you have any idea of the risk you have put us all in?

KEIKO: *(uncomfortably)* I didn't really *tell* her, Mom. I just mentioned that maybe—

IKU: Keiko, you have placed us all in great danger. If your father finds out—

KEIKO: *(pleading)* Mom, you can't tell him. You can't. Please. It was a mistake. I know that. But Marcy would never tell. She's my *friend*.

IKU: *(shaking her head)* Friendship is funny these days. And if she tells someone who isn't your friend, well . . .

(Susumu and Isamu enter the house. Susumu looks shaken and defeated. Isamu looks angry.)

IKU: You're home early. Is everything all right?

SUSUMU: *(sinking heavily into a chair)* No. Everything is not all right.

IKU: *(anxiously)* What happened?

SUSUMU: *(pulling out another paper from his pocket)* Oh, only that we are now not allowed outside of the house—at all.

ISAMU: *(angrily)* We can't very well carry messages to the Japanese government and bomb innocent Americans if we're inside our homes, can we?

KEIKO: So what about leaving? If we leave, will they arrest us?

SUSUMU: They might.

KEIKO: Maybe we should just stay here and not cause any trouble by trying to leave.

SUSUMU: No. We're going. Tonight. Maybe they don't have patrols out yet.

IKU: Patrols! For us? How can they? We've been in this community for years. We've built that business from the ground up, we—

SUSUMU: I know, I know. You've said all that before. But we have to get moving. We don't have time to sit around and chat. I'll move the car into the garage— surely they can't be angry at that—and we can pack it. In the meantime, pull down those shades. We don't want anyone to see what we're doing in here. You can't be too careful.

(Iku looks knowingly at Keiko, who lowers her head.)

ISAMU: I have about six boxes of stuff in my room. I'll carry it out.

SUSUMU: *(laughs shortly)* Six boxes! He thinks he's a king. Isamu, think for just a moment. If everyone has six boxes, how much room will there be for us? You can have one box. Everything has to go in the trunk or on the seats. We can't put boxes on the top. It's too risky.

IKU: *(looking helplessly at the items surrounding her in the room)* I can't bear this. Maybe we should stay. Do we leave behind the things our parents gave us? Do we bring clothing instead of photographs? This is our whole life, sitting here! How can we do this, just leave it behind?

SUSUMU: *(He goes over to her and puts his hands on her shoulders.)* Wife, I know this is difficult. This is one of the most difficult things we have ever done. But I heard more news today. They are readying the camps. They will be like prison camps, and we will have to go there and live as if we are in prison. We have no choice.

IKU: *(She bows her head and begins to cry quietly.)* Susumu, I feel like a criminal doing this.

SUSUMU: They are treating us as criminals.

KEIKO: *(gently)* Come on, Mother. I'll help you sort through things. *(Keiko takes her mother's hand and leads her to one of the piles on the couch.)*

ISAMU: *(to Susumu)* I hate to see Mother this way.

SUSUMU: *(sighs)* Better get your packing done.

ACT TWO, SCENE 2

The Goto family's garage and driveway leading to the street in front of their house, several hours later. The car is parked in the garage.

SUSUMU: *(to Keiko, as they fit the last few packages in* *odd corners of a car that appears already full)* The car can't hold another square inch. I think we'll be jamming our heads on the roof of the car. Iku? Iku? Are you ready?

IKU: *(We hear her voice from offstage, inside the house)* I can't—I just can't—

SUSUMU: *(impatiently)* You can't what? We need to get going.

IKU: *(in tears)* We shouldn't be doing this. Leaving everything. How can we? So much of our history. The pictures of Isamu and Keiko when they were small. The china. The first chair we bought—do you remember, Susumu, we were so excited to buy such a beautiful chair? All the food, and the children's books, and—

SUSUMU: *(gently)* I know, Iku. I know. I'm trying not to think about it. But the Hendersons have said they'll watch the house, and we'll be able to come back someday, when this war is over. We can trust the Hendersons. They'll watch over our things.

KEIKO: Mother, I know how you feel, but they're only things. We can get new things in Colorado.

ISAMU: When we get to Colorado and find jobs, I'm going to save up and buy you the best chair you've ever seen.

IKU: *(gathering her children to her)* Keiko, Isamu. Thank you. I hope in Colorado you won't be hurt the way you've been hurt here.

SUSUMU: *(looking at his watch)* I want to get going. Everything is packed. The house is locked up. Let's go. *(Isamu opens the garage door.)* Keiko, Isamu, let's push the car down the driveway. I don't want anyone to hear us and call the police.

IKU: *(shaking her head)* I never thought I would break the law.

(Isamu and Keiko slowly push the car down the driveway. When the car is at the end of the driveway, the family members silently get in the car, shutting the doors as quietly as they can. Susumu turns the key in the ignition. The car starts. At that moment, we hear sirens and see flashing lights, as two police cars roar to a stop in front of the driveway, blocking the car.)

IKU: *(gasping as she puts a hand to her mouth)* The police! What will we do?

SUSUMU: *(grimly)* Nothing. There is nothing we can do. Wait. We can wait.

(Patrolmen get out of the two cars and approach the Goto's car.)

PATROLMAN 1: Going for a little ride? Don't you know you people are not supposed to be out?

SUSUMU: I—We—

(Patrolman 2 walks around the car, peering inside.)

PATROLMAN 2: Yep, going for a little ride. Looks like they were planning to take a little ride out of state. Going back to Japan?

SUSUMU: We were just taking a ride.

PATROLMAN 1: *(sneering)* A ride. Right. We'll take you on another little ride. How about that? You're through sending messages to your little Jap friends overseas. Get out.

(The family members get out of the car. The patrolmen grab their arms and put two of the Gotos into the back of one patrol car, and two into the other. On the street, lights go on, and neighbors gather on the lawns, talking to each other as they watch the scene. Iku, Susumu, and Keiko have their heads bowed. Isamu shouts loudly at the crowd as the patrolman shoves him into the back of the patrol car.)

ISAMU: We're just as American as you! This is wrong! You know us! Are we disloyal?

(Several people on the lawns turn away from Isamu.)

PATROLMAN 1: Be quiet. You're lucky we didn't put handcuffs on you.

(The patrol cars speed away, sirens blaring.)

ACT THREE

Inside one of the barracks of the Amache Relocation Camp in Colorado. It is November 1942. There is one room, about 20 by 18 feet. There are four beds, two chairs, a table, a window. The Goto family is sitting on the chairs and the beds.

IKU: *(rubbing her hands over her shoulders)* I'm so cold, so cold. I never seem to get warm.

ISAMU: I can't get warm, either. If you couldn't see through the cracks in the walls, it might help.

SUSUMU: *(unhappily)* I've talked to the director again. He said he has hundreds of applications like ours from internees who want to live with friends and relatives. It didn't matter that the Makabes live in Colorado, he said.

(Isamu begins coughing a deep, hacking cough.)

IKU: Isamu. That cough. It hasn't gone away since we arrived here. I'm worried about you.

ISAMU: *(waving away his mother's concern)* Don't worry, Mother. I'm sure it will go away. Besides, everyone here has a cough or something else.

IKU: I know. This is no place for human beings to live. *(gesturing bitterly toward the window)* Look at that barbed wire outside. A guard house. What do they think we are going to do? This is shameful.

ISAMU: What I mind is all this wasted time. We just sit around, waiting to stand in food lines for hours. Think of what we could be doing.

IKU: Some of the other women have been told to form a fire brigade and carry heavy fire hoses. They don't seem interested in what we can do best.

KEIKO: They say they're going to start a school here next year.

IKU: Next year! If we're here next year, I will—I will—

SUSUMU: We may be here as long as the war lasts. All we can do is wait and hope that the authorities approve our application to live with the Makabes.

IKU: By then, Isamu might be dead!

KEIKO: Mother!

SUSUMU: Iku! Calm down! Isamu is not that sick.

IKU: I've heard coughs like that before. He needs to be somewhere warm, somewhere where people will take care of him. He needs good doctors. *(her voice rising)* There's no running water here! It's always cold! And

169

to look at that barbed wire every day would make anyone sicker!

SUSUMU: *(He grabs Iku by the arms and shakes her.)* Iku! You must stop this! We will work something out. If you lose hope, we all will. Now, stop it!

IKU: *(Her head is bowed, and she speaks woodenly.)* I am sorry.

KEIKO: Mother, you'll be OK. We all will. It is hard— being able to bring so little with us, feeling like the whole country hates us. But remember, there are people like the Hendersons. They'll take care of our things back in California.

ISAMU: *(coughing)* And there are other people, like whoever told the police we were leaving. Who would do that? How could they have known?

IKU: It doesn't matter now.

SUSUMU: The strange thing is that we end up in Colorado anyway. Instead of visiting our family in Denver, we're prisoners in a camp. Life goes in strange ways.

KEIKO: Why would the governor of Colorado let Japanese come here in camps while his own Japanese citizens are free outside?

SUSUMU: You know the order only applied to the Japanese on the West Coast. Besides, I hear from your aunt that the Colorado governor has taken the side of the Japanese in this.

KEIKO: Taken the side of the Japanese? Why are we in camps, then?

SUSUMU: They had trouble finding states that would let

Japanese in, even in camps. Governor Carr said it was fine to have a camp here. But he also said— Hanayo sent a newspaper article—that he didn't think any Japanese citizens should be locked up.

ISAMU: That does us a lot of good, doesn't it? *(He begins coughing again, a hacking cough that continues.)*

IKU: *(getting to her feet with her fists clenched)* This can't go on! I will go to the officials. I will threaten them if I must! Isamu needs help!

(Iku puts on a shawl and begins walking determinedly to the door. Susumu and Keiko quickly try to stop her.)

KEIKO: Mother, you must stop this! You must! There is nothing to be done!

(Iku and Keiko struggle.)

IKU: *(shouting)* You must not stop me! What can they do? Arrest me? Let me go!

(There is a knock at the door. Iku and Keiko let each other go.)

SUSUMU: Come in.

(The official enters.)

OFFICIAL: Are you the Goto family?

SUSUMU: *(rises)* Yes?

OFFICIAL: Pack your things. The Makabe family is taking you.

(Behind the official, a Japanese woman about the age of Iku rushes in.)

HANAYO: Iku! Susumu! Keiko! Isamu! *(She embraces

them.) Oh, I'm so sorry that it took so long. You know officials! But now you're safe. You can come with me. There's room for you all. Oh, I so wanted you to come, but not this way. Not this way.

IKU: *(in a wondering voice)* Is it true? Is it true?

OFFICIAL: *(nods)* Yes. You can go as soon as you finish the paperwork.

KEIKO: Now? Right now?

(The official nods again.)

(The family busies itself tying clothes into bundles and putting its few possessions into boxes. Iku looks around in a daze at the bare walls and the shabby room as the family packs up its belongings. The official waits. One by one, the family leaves the room. Iku is the last to leave.)

IKU: *(gazing at the small, bare room)* But what about all the other families here? The Noguchis are so unhappy in this place! And Mrs. Ogawa has the same cough that Isamu has, but she is nearly eighty!

SUSUMU: *(He returns with an anxious look on his face, overhears Iku, and speaks softly but urgently.)* We are lucky, very lucky. Come, before we annoy the officials.

(They hurry out together, Susumu guiding Iku with his arm around her shoulder. The official watches them passively, turns out the light, and closes the door.)

READING FOR UNDERSTANDING

Act One

1. How are people turning against Japanese Americans?

2. Why is Susumu eager to go to Iku's cousins in Colorado? At first, why do Iku and Keiko want to stay where they are?

3. What shows the son that the family is at risk in Los Angeles?

Act Two

4. Why is Iku upset when her daughter tells a friend about going to Colorado?

5. What new restriction makes the Gotos decide to flee?

6. Iku has doubts about leaving. What are they?

Act Three

7. In the camp, Iku points toward the barbed wire and guardhouse outside the window. What do these details reveal about the relocation camp? What other details tell you about life in the camp?

8. Why are the Gotos allowed to leave the camp?

RESPONDING TO THE PLAY

1. Think about the real events portrayed in the play. Did you know that Japanese Americans were "relocated" during World War II? How does this part of U.S. history affect your ideas about racism?

2. Some neighbors watched as police officers forced the Gotos into their patrol car. Imagine that you saw the Gotos arrested. Would you speak out?

Would you be silent? Describe in a paragraph what you think you would do.

3. Since the end of World War II in 1945, war has not touched U.S. soil. But the idea that there are enemies in the country still remains. Such views often exist despite evidence against them. Why do you think people have these ideas?

REVIEWING VOCABULARY

Match each word on the left with the correct definition on the right.

1. hooligans   **a.** to remove from an area
2. curfew   **b.** not showy or fancy
3. dramatic   **c.** people who do bad things
4. modest   **d.** in an exaggerated way
5. evacuate   **e.** rule that requires people to be off the streets at certain times

THINKING CRITICALLY

1. Prejudice against Japanese Americans grew stronger when the United States and Japan were at war. Why do you think war would increase prejudice? Can you think of other reasons why racism grows in a community or country?

2. In the play, some of Keiko's classmates turned against her. Her father also lost loyal customers. Why didn't these people show support? Do you think they acted out of fear or prejudice? Explain your answer.

3. Do you know anyone who has experienced prejudice because of nationality or race? How did this person respond? What do you think is the best way to respond?

WRITING PROJECTS

1. Imagine that *The Amache Trap* has a third act in which the Goto family returns to the old neighborhood in Los Angeles. Think of scenes that might take place, such as a reunion with their neighbors, the Hendersons, or a visit to Susumo's store. Write a scene with lines of dialogue and stage directions.

2. During her internment, Mrs. Goto probably wrote to her cousins in Denver. Write a letter from her point of view. Describe the conditions in the camp, her fears and hopes, and her plans for life after the war.

The Fruits of Protest

Carroll Moulton

Did you know that most U.S. fruit and vegetable growers rely on migrant workers to pick crops? Migrant workers are farm workers who move from place to place. They follow the harvest of crops. They struggle to make a living.

Many of the migrant workers are Mexican Americans. Many cannot speak English well. Some farm owners take advantage of them. They make the workers pick crops for very low wages. The workers are often cheated.

For many years, the situation was grim. Farm workers had no leaders to inspire them. There was no organization that could help them get justice and equality.

Finally, things began to turn around. Many African Americans had organized a civil rights movement in the 1950s and 1960s. Their successes inspired César Chávez and Dolores Huerta. These two people led the struggle for better wages and working conditions for migrant farm workers. The struggle, called la causa, *gave Mexican Americans new hope. Many took new pride in their culture and identity.*

This play takes place during 1967 and 1968, when many groups fought for equal rights. It was a time when everything seemed possible to a young Mexican American like Gloria. Gloria decided to join la causa. *But as you will see, her decision was not an easy one.*

VOCABULARY WORDS

barrio (BAHR-ee-oh) a Spanish-speaking neighborhood
❖ Mr. Ruiz owns a grocery store in the *barrio*.

sombrero (sahm-BRAIR-oh) a wide-brimmed Mexican hat
❖ The *sombrero* she wore protected her face from the blazing sun.

tortillas (tohr-TEE-yuhz) flat, round cakes of cornmeal or flour, baked on a griddle
❖ *Tortillas* are one of her family's favorite foods.

bungalow (BUN-guh-loh) small house or cottage
❖ A *bungalow* usually has two or three rooms.

boycott (BOI-kaht) refusal to buy, sell, or use something
❖ The laborers formed a national grape *boycott*.

KEY WORDS

campesinos (kahm-peh-SEE-nohs) Spanish word for *farm workers*
❖ *Campesinos* were paid less than factory workers.

chicana (chee-KAH-nah) female of Mexican descent (*chicano*—chee-KAH-noh—is male) who is a citizen or resident of the United States
❖ Being a *chicana*, Dolores Huerta was a leader with whom many of the farm workers could identify.

huelga (HWAIL-gah) Spanish for *labor strike*
❖ Gloria helped organize the famous *huelga* in 1965.

la causa (lah-KOW-sah) Spanish for *the cause*
❖ César Chávez urged involvement in *la causa*, the effort to improve salaries and working conditions for migrant farm workers.

178

CHARACTERS

Luis Rodriguez, *age seventeen*
Gloria Rodriguez, Luis's older sister, *age nineteen*
Lucinda Rodriguez, *age eleven*
Esteban Rodriguez, *age four*
Maria Rodriguez, *the children's mother*
Francisco Rodriguez, *the children's father*
Ruben Rodriguez, *age sixteen*
Rosa Sanchez, *head of the farm workers' credit union*
Epifanio Anaya, *a union organizer*
TV announcer

SETTING

Act One
Scene 1
The Rodriguez family bungalow, Delano, California, late October 1967

Scene 2
The bungalow, a few hours later

Act Two
Inside the headquarters building of the National Farm Workers Association (NFWA) in Delano, about seven months later: end of May 1968

Act Three
Outside the headquarters building, a week later, on the morning of Wednesday, June 5, 1968

ACT ONE, SCENE 1

*I**nterior of a two-bedroom bungalow** in the Mexican American barrio on the outskirts of the small valley town of Delano in south central California grape country. The time is late October 1967. These cramped*

179

quarters are home to the Rodriguez family: Francisco and Maria and their five children, who range in age from nineteen (Gloria) to four (Esteban). Francisco drives a truck for Giumarra Vineyards, the largest local grower of table grapes. He makes a better living than most Mexican Americans in Delano, who are mostly migrant workers, but he still must struggle to support his large family. Maria has often worked cleaning houses part time, but she usually has to stay home to take care of her young children. Gloria, the oldest child, is the hope of the Rodriguez family: smart, well-spoken, ambitious, athletic, strikingly pretty, and very independent-minded. After graduating from high school, she has found work in the fields at $1.15 an hour so that she can save up for college. In the off seasons, she does bookkeeping for a cement factory. Her brothers, Luis (seventeen) and Ruben (sixteen), are officially enrolled at Delano High School. Like dozens of Chicano children, however, they are truant during the picking season to help support the family. As the scene opens, we see Luis standing in front of a mirror, stage right, adjusting his necktie. He is dressed in his best clothes. Gloria sits at a large table covered with oilcloth, stage right, flipping the pages of a newspaper. It is about four o'clock on a Saturday afternoon.

LUIS: So, Gloria, aren't you going to Mass today?

GLORIA: Mass? How come you're going to Mass? Today's Saturday!

LUIS: Yeah, but we've got to pick tomorrow morning, Gloria. Mr. Halliday wants everyone out in the fields if the weather stays good. So Papa wants us all to go this afternoon.

GLORIA: *(sighing)* I guess I didn't get the word. OK,

well maybe I'll go with you guys. But I can always make it to the six-thirty mass tomorrow morning.

LUIS: *(The tie adjusted to his satisfaction, he starts to comb his hair intently.)* Yeah, and get an explosion from Dad. You know he has this thing about us all going to church as a family.

GLORIA: *(a little wearily)* I know, I know. *(looks at her watch)* Well, I've still got a whole hour to get ready.

LUIS: *(studying his hair critically)* Not if you get going after Ruben hits the bathroom! You'll be lucky to end up with five minutes in there.

GLORIA: Yeah, I know. That kid's on a wash cycle that lasts for hours. OK, just let me finish this article.

LUIS: What are you reading about, Gloria?

GLORIA: Oh, just an article in the Delano paper about Rosa Sanchez.

LUIS: *(Teasing, he crosses the stage and leans over Gloria's shoulder.)* You're always reading, Sis! Ruben may need a laundromat to make him happy, but you need a library to keep you happy. Who's Rosa Sanchez, by the way?

GLORIA: *(jokingly wagging her finger like a school-teacher)* Well, one reason I read stuff, brother of mine, is to find out what's going on in the big wide world, not to mention right here in Delano. Rosa Sanchez is head of the farm workers' credit union down at headquarters. *(respectfully)* She's one of Dolores Huerta's most important assistants.

LUIS: *(joking again)* So she's the one we have to see when we apply for a luxury car loan?

GLORIA: Yeah, she's holding the money bags. Seriously, though, Luis, you know the credit union's really important for a lot of families here in the barrio. Some of them couldn't buy the food they need without it.

LUIS: *(He shrugs and returns to the mirror.)* Yeah, I guess so, Gloria. I just never understand how economics works.

(Door opens from next room, and Lucinda, age eleven, enters, holding little Esteban by the hand. Both are dressed neatly for church: Esteban in shorts and a cowboy shirt, Lucinda in a colorful print dress. She wears a white satin ribbon in her hair and bright red shoes.)

LUCINDA: I finally got him dressed, Gloria. Isn't he handsome?

GLORIA: Why, look at you, Esteban! You are quite the little man! *(Esteban shyly covers his face with his hands and turns away from Gloria toward Lucinda.)*

LUIS: *(appraising his little brother's costume.)* Sharp, Esteban, very sharp. I'm going to get you a sombrero.

LUCINDA: Gloria, can I take him for a walk before Mama and Papa get back?

GLORIA: Good idea. If you pass by the store, pick up some beans from Mr. and Mrs. Paz and some cornmeal. I promised Mama I'd make tortillas for dinner tonight. Here's some money. And just make sure to get back here before five-thirty.

LUCINDA: No problem. I want to show Conchita my new dress! *(She does a few dance steps, singing as she nears the door.)* Come on, Esteban.

(They exit by the front door of the bungalow.)

GLORIA: *(after a brief pause)* Luis, are you serious about not knowing who Rosa Sanchez is? You really mean you never heard of her?

LUIS: *(now engaged in setting up the ironing board so he can iron his jacket)* Well, I can name all the musicians in every band in East L.A., Gloria. But no, I got to admit honestly that I've never heard of this Rosa Sanchez. Is she good-looking? Can you fix me up?

GLORIA: *(a little irritated)* Don't be silly, lover boy, she could be your mother. It's just amazing that you don't know about her, though, when she's right here in Delano. Doing things for our people, Luis, like getting the growers to stop using dangerous insecticides and helping laid-off pickers.

LUIS: Well, don't get so upset! Come on, now, tell me about her.

GLORIA: *(excitedly)* She grew up in Arizona, like César Chávez, and she's really close to Dolores Huerta. It says here that she'll probably go with both of them to the union's big new round of negotiations with the Teamsters to get their help in organizing the campesinos, or farm workers, as the unions call them. You can read the article. And I'll tell you more after I meet with her.

LUIS: You're going to meet with her?

GLORIA: *(She hesitates a moment, and then realizes she has said more than she meant to. Then she decides to trust her favorite brother.)* Monday morning at eight-thirty.

LUIS: So what are the two of you going to talk about?

GLORIA: *(casually)* I thought she might need a little help around the office. You know, Luis, I'm pretty good at that kind of stuff. I've been keeping the books for the cement company for nearly a whole year now.

LUIS: So you're going to get involved in the movement?

GLORIA: I don't know yet if they can use me. But yes, Luis, I want to get involved. Somebody has to. The campesinos picking out in the fields are still making only half the wages of the average factory worker. You're not blind. You get paid even less, and you can see for yourself how some of our people are living in the barrio. I've been thinking about this for a long time. Last month, I wrote Dolores Huerta a letter. I told her how much I admired the way she's led the movement while raising a family. Some of her kids worked in the huelga in 'sixty-five, you know.

LUIS: Didn't she get locked up a couple of times during the strike?

GLORIA: She's been in jail a lot, just like Chávez, just like Martin Luther King. Anyway, remember when Mr. Cole accused me of cheating on a biology exam in junior year because he didn't believe that a *chicana* could score so high? I told Dolores Huerta about that in my letter. And guess what? She wrote back that practically the same thing had happened to her in high school English class. She told me that if I wanted to get involved in the movement, I should go see Rosa Sanchez, right here in Delano.

LUIS: That's great, Gloria, but I don't think Papa's going to like it. You know that he and Mama have set their hearts on your becoming a doctor. How're you going to save any money for college if you work for these people? They don't pay their volunteers, you know.

GLORIA: Of course they don't pay volunteers, dummy. But I have to do what I feel is right in my heart. Now listen, Luis, promise me you won't say anything to Papa about this. I'm going to talk to him myself.

LUIS: OK, Gloria, but tell me when, so I can plan to be out of the room when you do it!

GLORIA: You think he's going to be that angry?

LUIS: *(nodding)* I don't *think* so, Gloria, I *know* so!

GLORIA: *(pauses a moment, then assumes a determined expression)* In that case, I'll tell him right after church.

(blackout)

ACT ONE, SCENE 2

Inside the bungalow, several hours later. As the lights go up, the front door opens. The Rodriguez family, led by Francisco, returns from church. They all scatter around the room, taking off hats, coats, and ties.

MARIA: I'm going to give you something special tonight, Esteban. You were so good in church!

GLORIA: You remember, I told you I'd make the tortillas tonight, Mama. *(to Lucinda)* Where'd you put that cornmeal?

LUCINDA: Right on the counter next to the stove.

FRANCISCO: Yes! Gloria's tortillas. It's our lucky day! You're the best cook in Delano, Gloria. After your mother, of course. *(After giving Maria a joking formal* *bow, he sits down in his favorite chair, puts on his reading glasses, and picks up a newspaper.)*

MARIA: I'll just change my dress, and then I'll help you, Gloria. Lucinda, please get Esteban out of his fancy clothes.

(The three of them exit into one of the bedrooms.)

LUIS: *(aside to Gloria)* So is now the time? You going to talk to him? *(She nods.)* Hey, Ruben, what do you say we take a hike over to Gary's? Let's see if we can get up a ballgame before dinner.

RUBEN: OK! Great idea! *(He grabs his mitt.)* When we going to eat, Gloria?

GLORIA: *(over her shoulder)* I'll give you guys an hour.

FRANCISCO: *(patting his stomach with a mock cry of despair)* Oh, come on, Gloria, we're starving! *(He chuckles.)* That's OK, boys. Have a good game, but don't keep us waiting all night for the tortillas.

(The boys pile out the door, leaving Gloria and Francisco alone together in the room.)

GLORIA: *(searching for a way to bring up the subject of her plans)* So, Papa, Father Ramirez was pretty good this afternoon, don't you think?

FRANCISCO: Yes, he was fine today. I like Ramirez. He's a good young priest. But when his sermons get so much into politics, he loses me, Gloria.

GLORIA: But don't you think the church needs to get into politics, Papa? You've always said that the church is part of our culture, and—

FRANCISCO: *(He puts down the paper and takes off his*

glasses.) Now listen, *mi hija*, the Mass is the Mass, except now it's in Spanish and not in Latin any more. But when the church gets into politics, it's wrong. That's one of the greatest things about America. Religion and government are separate, and that's the way they ought to be.

GLORIA: Well, you may be right about that, but—

FRANCISCO: *(sternly)* And what goes for the church goes for the Rodriguez family, Gloria. Now tell me, is it true what I hear in the barrio that you've been hanging around the NFWA building? What's going on?

GLORIA: *(a little taken aback, but relieved that she did not have to bring up the subject herself)* Well, Papa, I'd hardly call a visit or two to the farm workers' union headquarters building "hanging around." I want to talk to you, though. I've been thinking about getting more involved in *la causa*, Papa.

FRANCISCO: *(visibly upset, but trying to control himself)* You want to be in *la causa*, Gloria? What happened to our plans for you to go to college? To become a doctor?

GLORIA: I have my whole life for that, Papa. This is a really important time for the union. They need all the support we can give them.

FRANCISCO: We? Who's we?

GLORIA: *(with a trace of self-righteousness)* All of us, Papa, all our *chicano* brothers and sisters.

FRANCISCO: *(impatient)* Oh, Gloria, don't give me all that political stuff about "our people." That kind of talk can get people into a lot of trouble, especially around here. You know that your mother and I want

187

you to go to college in Fresno. Think about your education! We want you to have a better life than we've had when you grow up. We have dreams for you, Gloria.

GLORIA: Papa, I am grown up. And I think every day about a better life—not just for me, but for all our people, all the families.

FRANCISCO: *(suddenly shifting to a new tack)* Well, let's say that maybe you're not ready for a full schedule at college next year. Why don't you see if you can do some part-time modeling down in L.A.? *(flattering his laughter a bit)* Who knows? You're as pretty as Rita Moreno, you know. Prettier! And the extra money could help pay for your college expenses.

GLORIA: *(She sees right through his strategy and tosses her head impatiently.)* Don't be silly, Papa. *(adding with a touch of illogic)* Besides, Rita Moreno is not a *chicana*. She's from Puerto Rico.

FRANCISCO: So, she's still a *latina*, isn't she? Last time I looked, they spoke Spanish in Puerto Rico.

GLORIA: Papa, I don't *want* to model. You know that. You're just trying to change my mind about getting involved in social protest.

FRANCISCO:: *(hotly)* You're right! I'm trying to change your mind, Gloria! Leave that kind of thing to César Chávez. Now listen to me, Gloria. If you're not going to think about your family or your future, at least think about your own safety. There've been lots of attacks on union organizers. Probably more than what's been reported in the papers—

GLORIA: I'm a big girl, Papa. I can take care of myself.

FRANCISCO: *(rising out of his chair and finally losing his temper)* You may be an A student, Gloria, but just remember, you're only nineteen! You're thinking like somebody crazy! I'm telling you, I don't want you getting mixed up with those union people! And that's the end of the matter! *(He puts on his jacket and heads for the door.)*

GLORIA: Don't get so angry, Papa. Where are you going?

FRANCISCO: Out! Out to play dominoes. I've lost my appetite!

(He exits angrily, slamming the door behind him. After a moment, Maria enters from the bedroom.)

GLORIA: *(running over to her mother, very upset)* Oh, Mama, I'm so sorry! I had no idea he'd go so crazy over this—

MARIA: Calm yourself, Gloria. It's all right. He'll be back in an hour. You know he always wants to play dominoes with his buddies if he's worried about something. He's worried about you, Gloria.

GLORIA: Were you listening?

MARIA: *(nodding)* I heard. Now, Gloria, sit down and listen to your mother a minute. *(She takes Gloria by the hand, and they sit on the sofa together.)* You're a young woman now. Oh, I know Papa likes to pretend you're still a little girl, but you're going to have to make your decision as an adult. We just don't want you to get hurt, Gloria.

GLORIA: Mama, I know they sprayed insecticide on some of the strikers. There've been some beatings, but I'm going to be fine! They'll probably put me to

189

work as an office volunteer.

MARIA: *(thoughtful)* I know how much our people are suffering in *el barrio*, Gloria. You have a good heart, the way you want to help them. But there's something else—something that your father would never tell you.

GLORIA: What's that, Mama?

MARIA: *(quietly)* He's thinking of all of us. Papa's job might be in danger if the management at Giumarra finds out that a Rodriguez child is working for the workers' movement. There are others who've been fired, Gloria.

GLORIA: *(stunned)* But Mama, that's blackmail!

MARIA: *(She holds her daughter's hands in hers for a moment.)* It's life, Gloria. *(pauses and smiles a bit sadly.)* Oh, to be young again! *(collecting herself)* Your Papa and the boys'll be back soon. *(She rises and goes over to the stove.)* Let's start on the tortillas.

GLORIA: Yes, Mama. *(She stays seated for a moment, lost in thought, then gets up slowly and moves toward the stove to join Maria. Blackout.)*

ACT TWO

Headquarters building of the National Farm Workers of America (NFWA) in Delano. The union is still relatively small, and its headquarters is a one-story adobe building in the barrio. The scene is a simply furnished office with two desks, chairs, a single telephone, some battered file cabinets. Seven months have passed: a bright sunny morning in late May 1968. Gloria and Rosa Sanchez are studying a pile of papers at one of the desks.

Rosa Sanchez is a small, dark, dynamic woman in her late thirties.

ROSA: Now, Gloria, when we redo the application form, remember that we have to make it simpler. If people see too many questions on a form, they'll just give up on it completely. Understand?

GLORIA: Let me see if I can get it down to one page, Rosa. After all, we know that most of our loan applicants are good risks. Ninety percent of them live right here in the barrio.

ROSA: *(returning to sit at her own desk)* You've been a real help, Gloria. This office hasn't been the same since you got here. I really wish we could pay you, but the money situation is so tight right now.

GLORIA: Skip it, Rosa. Besides, you are paying me—by giving me a place to live. I couldn't afford more than two months in that rooming house after I moved out from home last fall. You saved the day when you told me you could give me a room in your house. And now that the national grape boycott's started, it's a lot more important to pay the workers that are organizing support for the boycott all over the country.

ROSA: Yeah, and from what Dolores says, they're doing a great job—even though all we can afford to pay them is five dollars a week. *(She pauses briefly to look down at some papers, then looks up again.)* Gloria . . .

GLORIA: Yes, Rosa?

ROSA: Have you talked to your father? Did you phone him like you said you were going to?

GLORIA: *(shaking her head)* Every time I pick up the phone, I try to think of the right words, and I can't dial the number.

ROSA: *(gently teasing)* You? At a loss for words? I don't believe it!

GLORIA: He just doesn't understand me, Rosa. And he hates anything that has to do with the workers' movement. Why, just before I left home, he actually said he thought the movement was probably full of communists.

ROSA: Well, that's hardly new. People said the same about the civil rights movement—*(dryly)* but they're saying it a lot less now, after Dr. King's assassination.

GLORIA: *(sighing)* Well, OK, Rosa, after I redo this form, I'm going to figure out how I can call Papa tonight. Maybe it'll help if I write down the first few words I want to say. *(She holds up a yellow pad and smiles.)* Something like an opening statement, huh?

(The telephone rings, and Rosa picks it up.)

ROSA: *(into phone)* National Farm Workers, Rosa Sanchez speaking. Yes, Dolores. Yes, I think so. I can be there at eleven if I leave right now. *(pause)* OK, I'll drive. See you soon. *(She hangs up the phone.)*

GLORIA: Time to hit the road again?

ROSA: *(reaching for her purse)* I have to get down to Bakersfield by eleven to drive Dolores to a rally. She wants to talk strategy on the way. You going to be OK here for the rest of the day? *(laughs)* Do you think you can find enough to do?

GLORIA: Sure, Rosa. I'll work on the loan form, and there's about forty-two other things to do, besides.

ROSA: *(As she opens the door to leave, she pauses to*

look over her shoulder at Gloria.) Times are rough, Gloria. There's Vietnam and race riots and bullets and people getting killed. We need all the family we can get. So make it forty-three things you've got to do today. Call your papa. *(She exits.)*

(Gloria buries herself in her work for a few moments. She looks up when she hears a knock at the door.)

GLORIA: Come in!

(Luis enters and walks quickly over to Gloria's desk.)

GLORIA: *(rising)* Luis, what brings you here? Aren't you supposed to be in school? Anyway, give me a hug!

(They hug warmly.)

LUIS: Hey, listen, I can only stay a minute, but I came over to tell you about the surprise birthday party we're planning for Papa.

GLORIA: Party?

LUIS: Yeah, you remember it's gonna be his fiftieth next Wednesday. *(He walks over to a big wall calendar and circles the date June 5.)* The fifth of June.

GLORIA: Luis, I've got a problem.

LUIS: Now come on, Gloria, I know you and Papa haven't been too close lately, but this is gonna be a special *fiesta*. All the neighbors are coming and Aunt Alicia and her kids and—

GLORIA: *(interrupting)* It's not what you're thinking, Luis. Anyway, I'm planning to give Papa a call tonight. But the problem is the date. June fifth is the beginning of the long march to Sacramento.

LUIS: So? Can't they march without you? Or can't you

catch up with them later?

GLORIA: You don't understand, Luis. They're counting on me. Something like this is really complicated. It's three hundred miles to Sacramento, and the march will be lasting twenty-five days. Chavez and Huerta are going to be along the whole way. There are all kinds of arrangements and preparations to be made. The day before the march is the primary election, and we'll be busy getting people out to vote, and—

LUIS: *(Now it is his turn to interrupt her.)* What I'm beginning to understand, Gloria, is that you're letting this movement take over your life. Papa's only going to be fifty once in his life, and you've gotta come, Sis!

GLORIA: *(torn)* I can't, Luis. I just can't!

LUIS: *(angrily walking to the door)* Well, I guess we aren't a family any more, are we? I'll see you around.

(He exits. After Luis closes the door, Gloria buries her face in her hands for a few moments. Then she picks up the yellow pad and a pencil.)

GLORIA: *(writing)* Hello, Papa?

(She pauses, lost in thought, as the lights fade slowly down.)

ACT THREE

Outside the small adobe NFWA headquarters in the barrio. Just before 9 A.M. on Wednesday morning, June 5, 1968. A pickup truck and several cars are parked on the street. A TV set has been set up outside the building on a high platform, and quite a few people are grouped in front of it, watching intently. Among them is Gloria Rodriguez. A crowd of farm workers, assembled to begin the long march to Sacramento, is milling around. Everyone is in shock from the news of Senator Robert Kennedy's assassination just after midnight in Los Angeles. Some workers are weeping openly; others are angry, shaking their fists as they talk together in small groups. Moments after the spotlights come up, a man climbs up to the platform. He is Epifanio Anaya, one of the regional union organizers.

EPIFANIO: Can we have a little quiet? I'm going to turn the volume up as loud as I can so that we can all hear.

(Calls of "Quiet." Crowd quiets down a bit.)

TV ANNOUNCER: *(voice rising)*. . . Sources close to the Kennedy family are now telling us that the body will be flown to New York City, where the Senator's funeral will be held at St. Patrick's Cathedral. He will then be laid to rest near his brother's grave in Arlington National Cemetery . . .

(The crowd watches in a stunned daze. Some of them make the sign of the cross in prayer. Rosa hurries onto stage. Spotting Gloria, she runs over to her.)

ROSA: Gloria, thank goodness I found you! Listen, I've just talked to Chávez in L.A. The march is still on. They've decided that Bobby Kennedy would've wanted it that way. So can you—

GLORIA: Was Chávez with him when he—?

ROSA: Yes, Gloria, César was calling from the Ambassador Hotel.

GLORIA: I still can't face it. It's a bad dream! First Dr. King, and now this! What's happening, Rosa?

ROSA: I don't know, Gloria. All I know is that I've got to get to Los Angeles right away. Chávez is planning to join the march in Fresno, and Huerta maybe sooner. Gloria, you've worked night and day setting up things for this march so it would run like a clock. I'm putting you in charge here.

GLORIA: But Rosa, I'm not—

ROSA: Yes, you are. You're one hundred percent quali- fied. And if you're not, you'll learn like all of us—by doing!

(She catches sight of Epifanio and pulls him over.)

Epifanio, the march is on. Help Gloria get their attention, and then she'll speak to them. Now I really have to run. *(She looks at everyone emotionally, kisses Gloria quickly, and exits.)*

EPIFANIO: You climb up on the pickup, Gloria, and grab the mike. I'll get them to be quiet.

(Epifanio circulates through the crowd of workers, telling them to pay attention. Gloria climbs into the back of the pickup truck and starts to speak.)

GLORIA: Listen, everyone! Our leaders still want us to march to Sacramento! Bobby may be gone, but his spirit's still alive in *la causa*. And César Chávez wants us to keep to our plan. You saw how people in California sent a message yesterday! Kennedy won the primary, and his victory was our victory.

(As she is speaking, Francisco enters stage right and walks slowly to the edge of the crowd.)

Bobby stood up for the *chicano* people and for our dreams. A lot of people thought *la causa* was crazy before he began to help us. So when we march, remember in your hearts what he used to say: Some people see things that are and ask, "Why?" I dream things that never were and ask, "Why not?" And remember: no violence. Now let's get started!

(Crowd reacts with applause and cheers. As they begin to move off stage in an orderly fashion to begin the march, Gloria climbs down from the pickup. Francisco remains behind, and father and daughter meet.)

FRANCISCO: Hello, Gloria.

GLORIA: Papa! *(shyly taking his hand)* Happy birthday, Papa.

FRANCISCO: *(hugging her)* Thank you, Gloria. That was quite a speech. I'm proud of you.

GLORIA: Proud, Papa?

FRANCISCO: Listen, Gloria, I've come to tell you something. All my life I've believed in certain things, and I haven't had too many doubts about what's important for me or my family. But today is different. Bobby Kennedy's dead. I can't believe it, but he's dead.

GLORIA: *(softly)* It's terrible, Papa.

FRANCISCO: The madness has to stop, Gloria. Today is truly a birthday for me because I'm beginning to understand a little better. People like me have to start getting involved. We can't sit on the sidelines any more, letting you youngsters carry all of the load. And we've got to be brave enough not just to hope for change, but to help make it happen.

GLORIA: *(smiling)* So you're thinking of helping the workers, Papa?

FRANCISCO: *(grinning back at her and wagging his finger)* Not so fast! But I will walk with you a little to find out more about this business. I will walk with you on the day of my birthday.

GLORIA: Oh, Papa! *(She hugs him tightly as the lights quickly fade down.)*

READING FOR UNDERSTANDING

Overview

1. Where does the action of the play take place?

2. What is *la causa*? Why does Gloria want to become involved in it?

3. Explain how Francisco Rodriguez comes to change his mind about his daughter's actions and about *la causa*.

Act One

4. How does Francisco feel about the church in America?

5. What profession does Gloria's family hope that she will enter?

6. At the end of this act, why do you think that Maria says "Oh, to be young again!"?

Act Two

7. What is Gloria's job at union headquarters?

8. Why do you think that Gloria starts writing, "Hello, Papa?" at the end of Act Two?

Act Three

9. Why does Rosa Sanchez put Gloria in charge of the march to Sacramento?

10. Near the end of the play, why does Francisco say: "Today is truly a birthday for me. . . "?

RESPONDING TO THE PLAY

1. Gloria puts off her career plans. She is at odds with her family. She does this to become involved in an issue that concerns her community and her people. Are there any current issues with which

you want to get involved? Explain your feelings in a brief diary entry.
2. By the end of the play, Gloria and her father seem to understand each other better. What do you think that parents and children can do to understand each other better? Write your suggestions in a paragraph.

REVIEWING VOCABULARY

Match each word on the left with its definition on the right.

1. sombrero
2. bungalow
3. barrio
4. tortillas
5. boycott

a. Spanish-speaking neighborhood
b. flat, round cakes
c. small house
d. refusal to buy or use a product
e. Mexican hat

THINKING CRITICALLY

1. What are Francisco's motives for urging Gloria not to get involved with *la causa?*
2. Do you think Gloria was right to disobey her father and join the movement? Why or why not?
3. Rosa Sanchez gave Gloria a place to live after she moved out. Yet Rosa says that it's very important for Gloria to find a way to make up with her father. Why do you think Rosa feels this way?
4. Do you think that Luis understands his sister Gloria very well? Why or why not?
5. If you had to predict what would happen to Gloria, how would you describe her life ten years after the end of the play?